Escaping Minimum Wage

Phillip D. Taylor, MS ED

an alumnus of Kent State University and The University of Akron.

Escaping Minimum Wage

Suggested Citation:

Taylor, Phillip, D. (2015). Escaping Minimum Wage. ProLineCareers.com, LLC: Akron, OH.

ISBN: 978-1503278318

Copyright © 2015 Phillip D Taylor
All Rights Reserved
1st Edition

To contact the author:

Write:
    Phillip D Taylor, MS ED
    1774 Horizon Dr—C
    Akron, OH 44313-8723

Email:
    Zantheffe@gmail.com

Website:
    www.ProLineCareers.com

Table of Contents

Preface		3
Chapter 1: History of the FLSA of 1938		4
History of MW Increases	20	
Minimum Wage by State	21	
Consumer Price Index	23	
Demographics of MW Workers	24	
Amount MW Should Be	25	
Summary & Conclusions	27	
Chapter 2: Arguments about the Minimum Wage		29
Arguments Against	29	
Arguments For	30	
Point & Counter-point	31	
Discussion of MW	38	
Typical Fast Food Restaurant	41	
Summary & Conclusions	43	
Chapter 3: Why You Can't Get Ahead		44
Food Stamps (SNAP)	49	
Median Income	51	
Reasons Why You Can't Get Ahead	54	
Summary & Conclusions	58	
Chapter 4: Poverty		59
Important Factors	61	
Economic Values	63	
Consequences of Inequality	65	
Where to Now	69	
Summary & Conclusions	69	
Chapter 5: Inventory of Resources		70
Class Standings	77	
Summary & Conclusions	79	

Chapter 6: Effective Education 82
- Educational Achievement 83
- Skill Level of Population 86
- Education Required for Entry 86
- Participation Rate 87
- Ratio of Jobs to Participants 87
- Jobs Requiring Less than HS 90
- Jobs Requiring HS Diploma 92
- Jobs Requiring Certificate 95
- Jobs Requiring Associate Degree 97
- Jobs Requiring Bachelor Degree 101
- Wide-Moat Professions 106
- Summary 107
- Conclusions 107

Chapter 7: Ownership 108
- Own a College Degree 110
- Own a Trade Skill 112
- Own the Ability to Sell 112
- Own the Ability to Communicate 113
- Own a Business 114
- Own a Home 115
- Own a Car 115
- Own Financial Instruments 116
- Own Your Life 117
- Summary 118
- Conclusions 119

Chapter 8: Practical Money Tactics 120
- Return on Investment 121
- Barriers to Wealth 122
- Money Personality 124
- List of Practical Money Tactics 125
- Summary 132
- Conclusions 133

Chapter 9: Remedies the Individual Can Take		134
List of Tactics	135	
Summary	140	
Conclusions	141	
Chapter 10: Remedies Society Can Take		142
Summary	148	
Conclusions	149	
Appendix A: Finding Your Purpose		150
Appendix B: Decision Making		152
Appendix C: Evaluate Possibilities		157
About the Author		162

"You must master a new way to think
before you can master a new way to be."
Marianne Williamson

Preface

Is a person less valuable if he or she is paid little for his or her time? How does someone escape the drudgery of a minimum wage job?

The short answers are: "No," and, "By adding value," respectively.

The answer is an emphatic "No." All work is honest and good if pursued with a purity of heart. Making minimum wage is nothing to be ashamed of. In fact, it the slothful man who should feel shame. Contributing to the best of your ability, where you are, and with what you have is all that is demanded from you. A man can only do what he can, and that, in the end, is enough.

And so, your obligation is to find an outlet for your best talent that someone is willing to pay for. This is the definition of work in its entirety. If we all used our best talent each day, there would be little we could not achieve.

As you will discover in later chapters, not only are more people working minimum wage jobs than ever before, but also, more people are moving up the career ladder than ever before. If you desire higher pay, with more responsibility, and less prescription of task, the only way to achieve this is by choice and resolve in making your skills more valuable in the workplace. No one can do it for you; this is something you have to do of your own accord. If you do it, you will succeed. If you do not, you remain stuck where you are, like an ant trapped in amber.

Minimum wage is just that, a minimum or a starting point. Getting beyond minimum wage requires you to increase your effectiveness in small jobs so when you are given bigger jobs, you do them well. Just like everything else in the world, you crawl before you walk. When do you say to the toddler, just give up trying to walk? After all, look at how many times you have failed. The obvious answer is you do not give up until. Until what? Until you make it.

Phillip D Taylor
Akron, Ohio
November 2014

Chapter 1

A History of FLSA of 1938

A quick history of the minimum wage law reveals the intent and story behind its arrival in America. There are several good histories of this law, but a particularly nice one is by Jonathan Grossman when he was historian for the U.S. Department of Labor. Below please find the complete discussion that originally appeared in the *Monthly Labor Review* of June 1978. The text in brackets is my commentary and is not part of the original document. This history is in the public domain.

www.dol.gov/dol/aboutdol/history/flsa1938.htm

On Saturday, June 25, 1938, to avoid pocket vetoes 9 days after Congress had adjourned, President Franklin D. Roosevelt signed 121 bills. Among these bills was a landmark law in the Nation's social and economic development -- Fair Labor Standards Act of 1938 (FLSA). Against a history of judicial opposition, the depression-born FLSA had survived, not unscathed, more than a year of Congressional altercation.

Escaping Minimum Wage

In its final form, the act applied to industries whose combined employment represented only about one-fifth [20%] of the labor force. In these industries, it banned **oppressive child labor** and set the **minimum hourly wage** at 25 cents, and the **maximum workweek** at 44 hours.1

Forty years later, a distinguished news commentator asked incredulously: "My God! 25 cents an hour! Why all the fuss?" President Roosevelt expressed a similar sentiment in a "fireside chat" the night before the signing. He warned: "Do not let any calamity-howling executive with an income of $1,000 a day, ...tell you...that a wage of $11 a week is going to have a disastrous effect on all American industry."2 [Today it's $15,000 per day vs. $290 per week or 260:1] In light of the social legislation of 1978, Americans today may be astonished that a law with such moderate standards could have been thought so revolutionary.

Courting disaster

The Supreme Court had been one of the major obstacles to wage-hour and child-labor laws. Among notable cases is the 1918 case of Hammer v. Dagenhart in which the Court by one vote held unconstitutional a Federal child-labor law. Similarly in Adkins v. Children's Hospital in 1923, the Court by a narrow margin voided the District of Columbia law that set minimum wages for women. During the 1930's, the Court's action on social legislation was even more devastating.3
New Deal promise. In 1933, under the "New Deal"
program, Roosevelt's advisers developed a National Industrial Recovery Act (NRA).4 The act suspended antitrust laws [i.e., Monopoly] so that industries could enforce fair-trade codes resulting in less competition and higher wages. On signing the bill, the President stated: "History will probably record the National Industrial Recovery Act as the most important and far-reaching legislation ever enacted by the American Congress." The law was popular, and one family in Darby, Penn., christened a newborn daughter Nira to honor it. 5

As an early step of the NRA, Roosevelt promulgated a President's Reemployment Agreement "to raise wages, create employment, and thus restore business." Employers signed more than 2.3 million agreements, covering 16.3 million employees. Signers agreed to a workweek between 35 and 40 hours and a minimum wage of $12 to $15 a week and undertook, with some exceptions, not to employ youths under 16 years of age. Employers who signed the agreement displayed a "badge of honor," a blue eagle over the motto "We do our part." Patriotic Americans were expected to buy only from "Blue Eagle" business concerns.6

In the meantime, various industries developed more complete codes. The Cotton Textile Code was the first of these and one of the most important. It provided for a 40-hour workweek, set a minimum weekly wage of $13 in the North and $12 in the South, and abolished child labor. The President said this code made him "happier than any other one thing...since I have come to Washington, for the code abolished child labor in the textile industry." He added: "After years of fruitless effort and discussion, this ancient atrocity went out in a day."7 [Today we have no Textile Industry after Off-shoring]

A crushing blow.

On "Black Monday," May 27, 1935, the Supreme Court disarmed the NRA as the major depression-fighting weapon of the New Deal. The 1935 case of Schechter Corp. v. United States tested the constitutionality of the NRA by questioning a code to improve the sordid conditions under which chickens were slaughtered and sold to retail kosher butchers.8 All nine justices agreed that the act was an unconstitutional delegation of government power to private interests. Even the liberal Benjamin Cardozo thought it was "delegation running riot." Though the "sick chicken" decision seems an absurd case upon which to decide the fate of so sweeping a policy, it invalidated not only the restrictive trade practices set by the NRA-authorized codes, but the codes' progressive labor provisions as well.9

As if to head off further attempts at labor reform, the Supreme Court, in a series of decisions, invalidated both State and Federal labor laws. Most notorious was the 1936 case of Joseph Tipaldo.10 The manager of a Brooklyn, N.Y., laundry, Tipaldo had been paying nine laundry women only $10 a week, in violation of the New York State minimum wage law. When forced to pay his workers $14.88, Tipaldo coerced them to kick back the difference. When Tipaldo was jailed on charges of violating the State law, forgery, and conspiracy, his lawyers sought a writ of habeas corpus on grounds the New York law was unconstitutional.

The Supreme Court, by a 5-to-4 majority voided the law as a violation of liberty of contract.11

[If a business can take advantage, will it?]

The Tipaldo decision was among the most unpopular ever rendered by the Supreme Court. Even bitter foes of President Roosevelt and the New Deal criticized the Court. Ex-President Herbert Hoover said the Court had gone to extremes. Conservative Republican Congressman Hamilton Fish called it a "new Dred Scott decision" condemning 3 million women and children to economic slavery.12

A switch in time.

Wage-hour legislation was a campaign issue in the 1936 Presidential race. The Democratic platform called for higher labor standards, and, in his campaign, Roosevelt promised to seek some constitutional way of protecting workers. He tried to pave the way for such legislation in his speeches and new conferences in which he spoke of the breakdown of child labor provisions, minimum wages, and maximum hour standards after the demise of the NRA codes.

When Roosevelt won the 1936 election by 523 electoral votes to 8, he interpreted his landslide victory as support for the New Deal and was determined to overcome the obstacle of Supreme Court opposition as soon as possible. In February 1937, he struck back at the "nine old men" of the Bench: He proposed to "pack" the Court by adding up to six extra judges, one for each judge who did not retire at age 70. Roosevelt further voiced his disappointment with the Court at the victory dinner for his second inauguration, saying if the "three-horse team [of the executive, legislative, and judicial branches] pulls as one, the field will be ploughed," but that the field will not be ploughed if one horse lies down in the traces or plunges off in another direction."13

However, Roosevelt's metaphorical maverick fell in step. On "White Monday," March 29, 1937, the Court reversed its course when it decided the case of West Coast Hotel Company v. Parrish.14 Elsie Parrish, a former chambermaid at the Cascadian Hotel in Wenatchee, Wash., sued for $216.19 in back wages, charging that the hotel had paid her less than the State minimum wage. In an unexpected turn-around, Justice Owen Roberts voted with the four-man liberal minority to uphold the Washington minimum wage law.

As other close decisions continued to validate social and economic legislation, support for Roosevelt's Court "reorganization" faded. Meanwhile, Justice Roberts felt called upon to deny that he had switched sides to ward off Roosevelt's court-packing plan. He claimed valid legal distinctions between the Tipaldo case and the Parrish case. Nevertheless, many historians subscribe to the contemporary view of Robert's vote, that "a switch in time saved nine."15

A young worker's plea

While President Franklin Roosevelt was in Bedford, Mass., campaigning for reelection, a young girl tried to pass him an envelope. But a policeman threw her back into the crowd. Roosevelt told an aide, "Get the note from the girl." Her note read,

I wish you could do something to help us girls....We have been working in a sewing factory,... and up to a few months ago we were getting our minimum pay of $11 a week... Today the 200 of us girls have been cut down to $4 and $5 and $6 a week. [Why didn't they quit? Because there was nothing else.]

To a reporter's question, the President replied, "Something has to be done about the elimination of child labor and long hours and starvation wages." [Yes, some businesses will take advantage, and some won't, but how do you separate the good from the bad?]
-Franklin D Roosevelt
Public Papers and Addresses, Vol. V
New York, Random House, 1936), pp. 624-25.

Back to the drawing board

Justice Roberts' "Big Switch" is an important event in American legal history. It is also a turning point in American social history, for it marked a new legal attitude toward labor standards. To be sure, validating a single State law was a far cry from upholding general Federal legislation, but the Parrish decision encouraged advocates of fair labor standards to work all the harder to develop a bill that might be upheld by the

Supreme Court.

An ardent advocate. No top government official worked more ardently to develop legislation to help underpaid workers and exploited child laborers than Secretary Frances Perkins. Almost all her working life, Perkins fought for pro-labor legislation. To avoid the sometime pitfall of judicial review, she consulted legal experts in forming legislation. Her autobiographical account of her relations with President Roosevelt is filled with the names of lawyers with whom she discussed legislation: Felix Frankfurter, Thomas Corcoran, Gerard Reilly, Benjamin Cohen, Charles Wyzanski, and many others both within and outside Government.

When, in 1933, President Roosevelt asked Frances Perkins to become Secretary of Labor, she told him that she would accept if she could advocate a law to put a floor under wages and a ceiling over hours of work and to abolish abuses of child labor. When Roosevelt heartily agreed, Perkins asked him, "Have you considered that to launch such a program... might be considered unconstitutional?" Roosevelt retorted, "Well, we can work out something when the time comes."[16]

During the constitutional crisis over the NRA, Secretary Perkins asked lawyers at the Department of Labor to draw up two wage-hour and child-labor bills which might survive Supreme Court review. She then told Roosevelt, "I have something up my sleeve....I've got two bills ... locked in the lower left-hand drawer of my desk against an emergency." Roosevelt laughed and said, "There's New England caution for you.... You're pretty unconstitutional, aren't you?"[17]

Earlier Government groundwork.

One of the bills that Perkins had "locked" in the bottom drawer of her desk was used before the 1937 "Big Switch." The bill proposed using the purchasing power of the Government as an instrument for improving labor standards. Under the bill Government contractors would have to agree to pay the "prevailing wage" and meet other labor standards. The idea had been tried in World War I to woo worker support for the war. Then, President Hoover reincarnated the "prevailing wage" and fair standards criteria as conditions for bidding for the construction of public buildings. This act -- the Davis-Bacon Act -- in expanded form stands as a bulwark of labor standards in the construction industry.

Roosevelt and Perkins tried to make model employers of government contractors in all fields, not just construction. They were dismayed to find that, except in public construction, the Federal Government actually encouraged employers to **exploit labor** because the Government had to award every contract to the lowest bidder. In 1935, approximately 40 percent of government contractors, employing 1.5 million workers, cut wages below and stretched hours above the standards developed under the NRA.

The Roosevelt-Perkins remedial initiative resulted in the Public Contracts Act of 1936 (Walsh-Healey). The act required most government contractors to adopt an 8-hour day and a 40-hour week, to employ only those over 16 years of age if they were boys or 18 years of age if they were girls, and to pay a "prevailing minimum wage" to be determined by the Secretary of Labor. The bill had been hotly contested and much diluted before it passed Congress on June 30, 1936. Though limited to government supply contracts and weakened by amendments and court interpretations, the Walsh-Healey Public Contracts Act was hailed as a token of good faith by the Federal Government -- that it intended to lead the way to better pay and working conditions.18

A broader bill is born

President Roosevelt had postponed action on a fair labor standards law because of his fight to "pack" the Court. After the "switch in time," when he felt the time was ripe, he asked Frances Perkins, "What happened to that nice unconstitutional bill you tucked away?"

The bill -- the second that Perkins had "tucked" away -- was a general fair labor standards act. To cope with the danger of judicial review, Perkins' lawyers had taken several constitutional approaches so that, if one or two legal principles were invalidated, the bill might still be accepted. The bill provided for minimum-wage boards which would determine, after public hearing and consideration of cost-of-living figures from the Bureau of Labor Statistics, whether wages in particular industries were below subsistence levels.

Perkins sent her draft to the White House where Thomas Corcoran and Benjamin Cohen, two trusted legal advisers of the President, with the Supreme Court in mind, added new provisions to the already lengthy measure. "Ben Cohen and I worked on the bill and the political effort behind it for nearly 4 years with Senator Black and Sidney Hillman," Corcoran noted.19

An early form of the bill being readied for Congress affected only wages and hours. To that version Roosevelt added a child-labor provision based on the political judgment that adding a clause banning goods in interstate commerce produced by children under 16 years of age would increase the chance of getting a wage-hour measure through both Houses, because child-labor limitations were popular in Congress.20

Congress-round I

On May 24, 1937, President Roosevelt sent the bill to Congress with a message that America should be able to give "all our able-bodied working men and women a fair day's pay for a fair day's work." He continued: "A self-supporting and self-respecting democracy can plead no justification for the **existence of child labor**, no economic reason for **chiseling worker's wages** or **stretching workers' hours.**" Though States had the right to set standards within their own borders, he said, goods produced under "conditions that do not meet rudimentary standards of decency should be regarded as contraband and ought not to be allowed to pollute the channels of interstate trade." He asked Congress to pass applicable legislation" at this session."21

Senator Hugo Black of Alabama, a champion of a 30-hour workweek, agreed to sponsor the Administration bill on this subject in the Senate, while Representative William P. Connery of Massachusetts introduced corresponding legislation in the House. The Black-Connery bill had wide Public support, and its path seemed smoothed by arrangements for a joint hearing by the labor committees of both Houses.
Generally, the bill provided for a 40-cent-an-hour minimum wage, a 40-hour maximum workweek, and a minimum working age of 16 except in certain industries outside of mining and manufacturing. The bill also proposed a five-member labor standards board which could authorize still higher wages and shorter hours after review of certain cases.

Proponents of the bill stressed the need to fulfill the President's promise to correct conditions under which "one-third of the population" were "ill-nourished, ill-clad, and ill- housed." They pointed out that, in industries which produced products for interstate commerce, the bill would **end oppressive child labor** and **"unnecessarily long hours** which wear out part of the working population while they keep the rest from having work to do." Shortening hours, they argued, would "create new jobs...for millions of our unskilled unemployed," and minimum wages would "underpin the whole wage structure...at a point from which collective bargaining [i.e., Unions] could take over." 22

Advocates of higher labor standards described the conditions of sweated labor. For example, a survey by the Labor Department's Children's Bureau of a cross section of 449 children in several States showed nearly one-fourth of them working 60 hours or longer a week and only one-third working 40 hours or less a week. The median wage was slightly over $4 a week.23

One advocate, Commissioner of Labor Statistics Isador Lubin, explained to the joint Senate-House committee that during depressions the ability to overwork employees, rather than efficiency, determined business success. The economy, he reported, had deteriorated to the chaotic stage where employers with high standards were forced by cut-throat competition to exploit labor in order to survive. "The outstanding feature of the proposed legislation," Lubin said, is that "it aims to establish by law a plane of competition far above that which could be maintained in the absence of government edict." 24

Opponents of the bill charged that, although the President might damn them as "economic royalists and sweaters of labor," the Black-Connery bill was "a bad bill badly drawn" which would lead the country to a "tyrannical industrial dictatorship." They said New Deal rhetoric, like "the smoke screen of the cuttle fish," diverted attention from what amounted to socialist planning. Prosperity, they insisted, depended on the "genius" of American business, but how could business "find any time left to provide jobs if we are to persist in loading upon it these everlastingly multiplying governmental mandates and delivering it to the mercies of multiplying and hampering Federal bureaucracy?"25

Organized labor supported the bill but was split on how strong it should be. Some leaders, such as Sidney Hillman of the Amalgamated Clothing Workers Union and David Dubinsky of the International Ladies' Garment Workers' Union, supported a strong bill. In fact, when Southern congressmen asked for the setting of lower pay for their region, Dubinsky's union suggested lower pay for Southern congressmen. But William Green of the American Federation of Labor (AFL) and John L. Lewis of the Congress of Industrial Organization (CIO), on one of the rare occasions when they agreed, both favored a bill which would limit labor standards to low-paid and essentially unorganized workers. Based on some past experiences, many union leaders feared that a minimum wage might become a maximum and that wage boards would intervene in areas which they wanted reserved for labor-management negotiations. They were satisfied when the bill was amended to exclude work covered by collective bargaining.

The weakened bill passed the Senate July 31, 1937, by a vote of 56 to 28 and would have easily passed the House if it had been put to a vote. But a coalition of Republicans and conservative Democrats bottled it up in the House Rules Committee. After a long hot summer, Congress adjourned without House action on fair labor standards.26

Congress-round II

An angry President Roosevelt decided to press again for passage of the Black-Connery bill. Having lost popularity and split the Democratic Party in his battle to "pack" the Supreme Court, Roosevelt felt that attacking abuses of child labor and sweatshop wages and hours was a popular cause that might reunite the party. A wage-hour, child-labor law promised to be a happy marriage of high idealism and practical politics.

On October 12, 1937, Roosevelt called a special session of Congress to convene on November 15. The public interest, he said, required immediate Congressional action: "The **exploitation of child labor** and the **undercutting of wages and the stretching of the hours of the poorest paid workers** in periods of business recession has a serious effect on buying power."27

Despite White House and business pressure, the conservative alliance of Republicans and Southern Democrats that controlled the House Rules Committee refused to discharge the bill as it stood. Congresswoman Mary Norton of New Jersey, now chairing the House Labor Committee, made a valiant attempt to shake the bill loose".28 Many representatives had told her that they agreed with the principles of the bill but that they objected to a five-man wage board with broad powers. Therefore, Norton told the House of Representatives that the Labor Committee would offer an amendment to change the administration of the bill from a five-man board to an administrator under the Department of Labor. Urging representatives to sign a petition to jar the bill out of committee, Norton appealed:

I now hope and urge that these Members will keep faith with me, as I have kept faith with them, and sign the petition . . . we are approaching Thanksgiving Day, . . . I do not see how any Member of this House can enjoy his Thanksgiving dinner tomorrow if he fails to put his name to that petition this afternoon.

Though Norton missed her Thanksgiving Day dead-line, by December 2, the bill's supporters had rounded up enough signers to give the petition the 218 signatures necessary to bring the bill to a vote on the House floor.29

With victory within grasp, the bill became a battle-ground in the war raging between the AFL and the CIO. The AFL accused the Roosevelt Administration of favoring industrial over craft unions and opposed wage-board determination of labor standards for specific industries. Accordingly, the AFL fought for a substitute bill with a flat 40-cent-an-hour minimum wage and a maximum 40-hour week.

In the ensuing confusion, shortly, before the Christmas holiday of 1937, the House by a vote of 218 to 198 unexpectedly sent the bill back to the Labor Committee.30 In her memoir of President Roosevelt, Frances Perkins wrote:

This was the first time that a major administration bill had been defeated on the floor of the House. The press took the view that this was the death knell of wage-hour legislation as well as a decisive blow to the President's prestige.31

Roosevelt tries again

Again, Roosevelt returned to the fray. In his annual message to Congress on January 3, 1938, he said he was seeking "legislation to end starvation wages and intolerable hours." He paid deference to the South by saying that "no reasonable person seeks a complete uniformity in wages." He also made peace overtures to business by pointing out that he was forgoing "drastic" change, and he appeased organized labor, saying that "more desirable wages are and should continue to be the product of collective bargaining."32

The day following Roosevelt's message, Representative Lister Hill, a strong Roosevelt supporter, won an Alabama election primary for the Senate by an almost 2-to-1 majority over an anti-New Deal congressman. The victory was significant because much of the opposition to wage-hour laws came from Southern congressmen. In February, a national public opinion poll showed that 67 percent of the populace favored the wage-hour law, with even the South showing a substantial plurality of support for higher standards.33

Reworking the bill.

In the meantime, Department of Labor lawyers worked on a new bill. Privately, Roosevelt had told Perkins that the length and complexity of the bill caused some of its difficulties. "Can't it be boiled down to two pages?" he asked. Lawyers trying to simplify the bill faced the problem that, although legal language makes legislation difficult to understand, bills written in simple English are often difficult for the courts to enforce. And because the wage-hour, child-labor bill had been drafted with the Supreme Court in mind, Solicitor Labor Gerard Reilly could not meet the President's two-page goal; however, he succeeded in cutting the bill from 40 to 10 pages.

In late January 1938, Reilly and Perkins brought the revision to President Roosevelt. He approved it, and the new bill went to Congress.34

Roosevelt and Perkins prepared for rugged opposition. Roosevelt put pressure on Congressmen who had ridden his coattails to election victory in 1936 and who then knifed New Deal legislation. Perkins added to her staff Rufus Pole, a young lawyer, to follow the bill through Congress. Pole worked resourcefully pinpointed the issues that bothered some Congressmen, and identified a large number of Senators and Representatives who could be counted on to vote favorably.

Norton appointed Representative Robert Ramspeck of Georgia to head a subcommittee to bridge the gap between various proposals. The subcommittee's efforts resulted in the Ramspeck compromise which Perkins felt "contained the bare essentials she could support."35 The compromise retained the 40-cent minimum hourly wage and the 40-hour maximum workweek. It did not provide for an administrator as had the previous bill which had been voted back to the committee by the House. Instead, the compromise allowed for a five-member wage board which would be less powerful than those proposed by the Black-Connery bill.

Congress-the final round

The House Labor Committee voted down the Ramspeck compromise, but, by a 10-to-4 vote, approved an even more "barebones" bill presented by Norton. Her bill following the AFL proposal, provided for a 40-cent hourly minimum wage, replaced the wage boards proposed by the Ramspeck compromise with an administrator and advising commission, and allowed for procedures for investigation into certain cases.36

A message from the voters. Again, the House Rules Committee (under Rep. John J. O'Conner of New York, whom Roosevelt called an "obstructionist" who "pickled" New Deal programs) prevented discussion of the bill on the House floor by a vote of 8 to 6.37 The President then put his prestige on the line. On April 30, 1938, for the sixth time since taking office, he communicated with Congress over wages and hours through a letter to Mrs. Norton. He said he had no right whatsoever as President to criticize the rules but suggested as an ex-legislator and as a friend that "the whole membership of the legislative body should be given full and free opportunity to discuss [exceptional measures] which are of undoubted national importance because they relate to major policies of Government and affect the lives of millions of people."

He avoided judgment of the bill but noted that the Rules Committee, by a narrow vote, had prevented 435 members from "discussing, amending, recommitting, defeating or passing some kind of a bill." He concluded: "I still hope that the House as a whole can vote on a wage and hour bill. ...I hope that the democratic processes of legislation will continue."38

Three days later, May 3, 1938, Congressman Claude Pepper won a resounding victory over anti-New Dealer J. Mark Wilcox in the Florida Senate primary. Wilcox had made New Deal programs the major issue and had labeled Pepper "Roosevelt rubber stamp."

Nothing impresses Congressmen more than election returns. The January and May victories of New Deal advocated in the South brought home to Southern Congressmen the message of how their constituents felt about fair labor standards. A petition to discharge the bill from the Rules Committee was placed on the desk of the Speaker of the House on May 6, at 12 noon. In 2 hours and 20 minutes, 218 members has signed it, and additional members were waiting in the aisles.39

Braving the floor battle. Proponents of the wage-hour, child-labor bill pressed the attack. They continued to point to "horror stories." One Congressman quoted a magazine article entitled "All Work and No Pay" which told how, in a company that paid wages in scrip for use in the company store, pay envelopes contained nothing for a full week's work after the deduction of store charges.

The most bitter controversy raged over labor standards in the South. "There are in the State of Georgia," one Indiana Congressman declaimed, "canning factories working ... women 10 hours a day for $4.50 a week. Can the canning factories of Indiana and Connecticut of New York continue to exist and meet such competitive labor costs?"40 Southern Congressmen, in turn, challenged the Northern "monopolists" who hypocritically "loll on their tongues" words like "slave labor" and "sweatshops" and support bills which sentence Southern industry to death. Some Southern employers told the Department of Labor that they could not live with a 25-cent-an-hour minimum wage. They would have to fire all their people, they said. Adapting a biblical quotation, Representative John McClellan of Arkansas rhetorically asked, "What profiteth the laborer of the South if he gain the enactment of a wage and hour law -- 40 cents per hour and 40 hours per week -- if he then lose the opportunity to work?"41

Partly because of Southern protests, provisions of the act were altered so that the minimum wage was reduced to 25 cents an hour for the first year of the act. Southerners gained additional concessions, such as a requirement that wage administrators consider lower costs of living and higher freight rates in the South before recommending wages above the minimum.

Though the revised bill had reduced substantially the administrative machinery provided for in earlier drafts, several Congressmen singled out Secretary Perkins for personal attack. One Perkins detractor noted that, although Congress had "overwhelmingly rebelled" against delegation of power,

We delegate to Madam Perkins the authority and power to 'issue an order declaring such industry to be an industry affecting commerce.' Now section 9 is ...one of the 'snooping' sections of the bill. Imagine the feeling of the merchant or the industry up in your district when a 'designated representative'...of Mme. Perkins' enter and inspect such places and such records'...I know no previous law going quite so far.42

A resulting compromise modified the authority of the administrator in the Department of Labor. The bill was voted upon May 24, 1938, with a 314-to-97 majority. After the House had passed the bill, the Senate-House Conference Committee made still more changes to reconcile differences. During the legislative battles over fair labor standards, members of Congress had proposed 72 amendments. **Almost every change sought exemptions, narrowed coverage, lowered standards, weakened administration, limited investigation, or in some other way worked to weaken the bill.**

The surviving proposal as approved by the conference committee finally passed the House on June 13, 1938, by a vote of 291 to 89. Shortly there-after, the Senate approved it without a record of the votes. Congress then sent the bill to the President. On June 25, 1938, the President signed the Fair Labor Standards Act to become effective on October 24, 1938.43 [It is quite messy, but it is the best system we have so far.]

Jonathan Grossman was the Historian for the U.S. Department of Labor. Henry Guzda assisted. This article originally appeared in the *Monthly Labor Review* of June 1978. The final section, titled "The act as law" and containing dated material, has been omitted in the electronic version.

"We have a system that increasingly
taxes work and subsidizes nonwork."
Milton Friedman

Escaping Minimum Wage

What is Minimum Wage?

From www.dol.gov/whd/minwage/chart.htm, we get the progression of minimum wage since its conception in 1938.

October 1938	$0.25
October 1939	$0.30
October 1945	$0.40
January 1950	$0.75
March 1956	$1.00
September 1961	$1.15
September 1963	$1.25
February 1967	$1.40
February 1968	$1.60
May 1974	$2.00
January 1975	$2.10
January 1976	$2.30
January 1978	$2.65
January 1979	$2.90
January 1980	$3.10
January 1981	$3.35
April 1990	$3.80
April 1991	$4.25
October 1996	$4.75
September 1997	$5.15
July 2007	$5.85
July 2008	$6.55
July 2009	$7.25

Current Minimum Wage as determined by individual states, which are free to legislate rates higher than the federal minimum, but not any lower. If a state legislates a rate lower than the federal rate, then the federal rate takes control. Data from Wikipedia.com.

Alabama	NA
Alaska	$7.75
Arizona	$7.90
Arkansas	$6.25
California	$9.00

Escaping Minimum Wage

Colorado	$8.00
Connecticut	$8.70
Delaware	$7.75
Florida	$7.93
Georgia	$5.15
Hawaii	$7.25
Idaho	$7.25
Illinois	$8.25
Indiana	$7.25
Iowa	$7.25
Kansas	$7.25
Kentucky	$7.25
Louisiana	NA
Maine	$7.50
Maryland	$7.25
Massachusetts	$8.00
Michigan	$8.15
Minnesota	$8.00
Mississippi	NA
Missouri	$7.50
Montana	$7.90
Nebraska	$7.25
Nevada	$8.25
New Hampshire	$7.25
New Jersey	$8.25
New Mexico	$7.50
New York	$8.00
North Carolina	$7.25
North Dakota	$7.25
Ohio	$7.95
Oklahoma	$7.25
Oregon	$9.10
Pennsylvania	$7.25
Rhode Island	$8.00
South Carolina	NA
South Dakota	$7.25

Escaping Minimum Wage

Tennessee	NA
Texas	$7.25
Utah	$7.25
Vermont	$8.73
Virginia	$7.25
Washington	$9.32
West Virginia	$7.25
Wisconsin	$7.25
Wyoming	$5.15

Selected Minimum Wage by Country in 2014 U.S. Dollars from Wikipedia.com.

Australia	$17.39
France	$12.22
UK	$10.32
Canada	$10.00
Japan	$8.48
USA	$7.25
Spain	$5.57
South Korea	$4.63
Saudi Arabia	$3.85
Brazil	$2.11
China	$1.19
Russia	$1.04
Syria	$1.02
Mexico	$0.61
Afghanistan	$0.57
Pakistan	$0.51
Venezuela	$0.34
Vietnam	$0.30
India	$0.28
Cuba	$0.05
Uganda	$0.01

Escaping Minimum Wage

The Consumer Price Index (CPI) is one way of measuring inflation across the United States. It is composed of prices paid by consumers in over 200 goods and services. Below are year-over-year increases in selected categories (September 2013 to September 2014).

Food
- Meat, Fish, Poultry, Eggs — 9.4%
- Food away from home — 2.7%
- Fruit & Vegetables — 0.9%

Housing
- Rent — 3.3%
- Owner's Equivalent Rent — 2.7%
- Water/Sewer/Trash — 3.8%

Clothing
- Men and Boy's Apparel — (0.4%)
- Women and Girl's Apparel — 0.4%

Transportation
- New Vehicles — 0.3%
- Used Vehicles — (0.4%)
- Gasoline — (3.6%)

Medical — 2.0%
Recreation — 0.1%
College Tuition — 3.2%
Telephone — (0.1%)
Tobacco — 2.0%
Personal Care Products — 1.3%

We can use the CPI to judge inflation over time. A 1967 dollar is worth $0.14 in 2014 dollars, a loss of 86% or 1.83% per year. A 1983 dollar is worth $0.42 in 2014 dollars, a loss of 58% or 1.93% per year. If we express minimum wage as a function of the CPI, then the 1967 minimum wage ($1.40) plus CPI inflation equals $10.00 in 2014, and the 1983

minimum wage ($3.35) plus CPI inflation equals $7.98. This represents a loss of buying power of 38% and 10% in 2014 dollars, respectively. From this data we can say that those incumbents working for minimum wage have experienced losses in real buying power because minimum wage has not increased with CPI inflation. Those working for minimum wage are increasingly being left behind.
Data from: www.bls.gov/cpi/cpid1409.pdf

Demographics and Related Statistics
   Typical incumbents working for minimum wage:
      64% are women
      70% are single
      20% are married
      10% are widowed or divorced
      51% are aged 16-24
      20% are aged 25-34
      11% are aged 35-44
      10% are aged 45-54
      5% are aged 55-64
      3% are aged 65+
      44% work for restaurants
      22% work in office & sales occupations
      18% work in personal services occupations
      64% possess a high school diploma or some college
      7% possess a bachelor degree or higher
      67% work part-time
   Over all only 4.7% of 76 million incumbents work for minimum wage
   The three sectors employing the least number of incumbents at minimum wage are: Construction, Mining, and Federal Government.

In this final section, we begin to examine the question, "What amount should minimum wage be?" In the history of minimum wage, its level was initially set at a multiple of the cost of food. We could also use a more arbitrary number like 50% (i.e., the 25th percentile of all workers) of the Median Wage for all workers, which is $9.54. Comparing the current minimum wage of $7.25 to the median income of $39,686, we arrive at about 38%. However, an easier and more fair determination of minimum wage is that point where a single person could work full-time and not need any form of public assistance. This would include Supplemental Nutrition Assistance Program (SNAP) (aka. Food Stamps), Earned Income Tax Credit (EITC), and Temporary Assistance to Needy Families (TANF) (aka. Welfare). As it stands now, an incumbent working full-time at $7.25 would be eligible to receive about $100 per month in food assistance.

Profitable corporations like Wal-Mart, McDonalds, and Choice Hotels effectively receive a subsidy to keep wages low. That is, since they pay incumbents the low going rate of minimum wage and the government supplies wealth transfer payments in programs described above, these corporations do not directly bear the full cost of their labor usage. In other words, companies that pay minimum wage are encouraged to pay as little as possible (not relative to productivity) since they know their employees will be taken care of by the government regardless. Companies paying minimum wage get an effective subsidy of $1.97 per hour for each incumbent making minimum wage and working full-time. Based on these data, an incumbent working full-time needs to earn about $19,169 or $9.22 per hour to make enough to live without any governmental assistance. This, I believe, is where minimum wage should be set, and routinely adjusted to going forward.

Where is our sense of dignity if an able-bodied man or woman with a high school diploma can work full-time at one of these good corporations, yet still need to collect a hand-out, public or private, just to survive?

Summary & Conclusions

Reasons Minimum Wage was made into law
    a. **Exploitation of Child Labor**
    b. **Exploitation of Adult Labor**
    c. **Cutting of Wages**
    d. **Unnecessary Long Hours**
[Notice reducing poverty was not an original purpose of the law.]

Amount Minimum Wage is and should be
    a. $7.25 is the current minimum since July 2009
    b. Using 1967 CPI we get $10.00
    c. Using 1983 CPI we get $7.98
    d. Using 50% of Median Income we get $9.54
    d. Using an amount where incumbent is totally self-sufficient (i.e., no government assistance), we get $9.22

NOTES

1. The New York Times, June 27, 28, 1938; Harry S. Kantor, "Two Decades of the Fair Labor Standards Act," Monthly Labor Review, October 1958, pp. 1097-98.
2. Franklin Roosevelt, Public Papers and Address, Vol. VII (New York, Random House, 1937), p.392.
3. Hammer v. Dagenhart, 247 U.S. 251 (1918); Adkins v. Children's Hospital, 262 U.S. 525 (1923).
4. The proper initials for the Law are NIRA. The initials for the National Recovery Administration created by the act as NRA. Following a common practice, the initials NRA are used here for both the law and the administration.
5. Roosevelt, Public Papers, II (June 16, 1933), p.246.
6. Roosevelt, Public Papers, II (July 24 and 27, 1933), pp. 301, 308-12.
7. Roosevelt, Public Papers, II (July 9 and 24, 1933), pp. 275, 99; Frances Perkins, The Roosevelt I Knew (New York, Viking Press, 1946); pp. 204-08.
8. Schechter Corp. v. United States, 295 U.S. 495(1935).
9. Arthur M. Schlesinger, The Age of Roosevelt (Boston, Mass., Houghton-Mifflin Co., 1960), pp. 277-83; Roosevelt, Public Papers, IV (May 29, 1935), pp. 198-221; John W. Chambers, "The Big Switch: Justice Roberts and the Minimum-Wage Cases," Labor History, Vol. X, Winter 1969, pp.49-52.
10. Morehead v. Tipaldo, 298 U.S. 587 (1936).
11. Ironically, like the four Schechter brothers in the NRA case who went broke, Tipaldo also suffered financially. "My customers wouldn't give my drivers their wash," he lamented. Columnist Heywood Broun quipped.

"Those who live by the chisel will die under the hammer." Chambers, "Big Switch," p. 57.

12. Chambers, "Big Switch," pp. 54-58.

13. Roosevelt, Public Papers, VI (Feb. 5 1937), pp. 51-59; VI (Mar. 4, 1937), p. 116; George Martin, Madam Secretary Frances Perkins(Boston Mass., Houghton-Mifflin Co., 1976), pp. 388-90.

14. West Coast Hotel Company v. Parrish, 300 U.S. 379 (1937).

15. Chambers, "Big Switch," pp. 44, 73; Robert P. Ingalls, "New York and the Minimum-Wage Movement, 1933-1937," Labor History, Vol. XV, Spring 1974, pp. 191-97.

16. Perkins, Roosevelt, p. 152

17. Perkins, Roosevelt, pp. 248-49, 252-53; Roosevelt, Public Papers, V (Jan.` 3, 1936), p. 15; Jonathan Grossman with Gerard D. Reilly, Solicitor of Labor, Oct. 22, 1965.

18. 25th Annual Report, Fiscal Year 1937 (U.S. Department of Labor), pp. 34-35; Herbert C. Morton, Public Contracts and Private Wages: Experience Under the Walsh-Healey Act(Washington, D.C., The Brookings Institution, 1965), pp. 7-10; The Department of Labor (New York, Praeger Publishers, 1973), pp. 19-20, 211-13.

19. Letter from Thomas Corcoran to Jonathan Grossman, Ap. 10, 1978.

20. Perkins, Roosevelt, pp. 254-57; Roosevelt, Public Papers, V(Jan. 7, 1937); Jeremy P. Felt, "The Child Labor Provisions of the Fair Labor Standards Act," Labor History , Vol. XI, Fall 1970, pp. 474-75; Interview, Jonathan Grossman with Gerard D. Reilly, Solicitor of Labor, Oct. 22, 1965.

21. Roosevelt, Public Papers, VI(May 24, 1937), pp. 209-14.

22. Record of the Discussion before the U.S. Congress on the FLSA of 1938, I.(U.S. Department of Labor, Bureau of Labor Statistics) (Washington, GAO, 1938), pp.20-21.

23. Hearings to Provide for the Establishment of Fair Labor Standards in Employments in and Affecting Interstate Commerce and for Other Purposes, Vol. V.(1937). (U.S. Congress, Joint Committee on Education and Labor, 75th Cong., 1st sess), pp. 383-84.

24. Isador Lubin, Testimony, Hearings to Provide Fair Labor Standards (1937), pp.309-10.

25. Record of Discussion of FLSA of 1938, I(U.S. Department of Labor),

pp.38, 115, 124.

26. Perkins, Roosevelt, pp. 257-59; Paul Douglas and Joseph Hackman, "Fair Labor Standards Act, I," "Political Science Quarterly Vol. LIII, December 1938, pp. 500-03, 508; The New York Times, Aug. 18, 1937.

27. Roosevelt, Public Papers, VI (Oct. 4, 1937, Oct. 12, 1937, Nov. 15, 1937), pp. 404, 428-29, 496

28. Mrs. Norton replaced Representative Connery as chair of the House Labor Committee after his death.

29. Record of Discussion of FLSA of 1938, (U.S. Department of Labor), (1937), p. 415.

30. The New York Times, Dec. 13, 1937; Douglas and Hackman, "FLSA," pp.508-11.

31. Perkins, Roosevelt, p. 261.

32. Roosevelt, Public Papers, VII (Jan. 3, 1938), p.6.

33. The New York Times, Jan. 5, Feb. 16, May 9, 1938.

34. Perkins, Roosevelt, p. 261.

35. Roosevelt, public Papers, VII (Aug. 16, 1938), pp. 488-89; Perking, Roosevelt, pp. 262-63.

36. Roosevelt, Public Papers, VI (May 24, 1937), pp. 215; Perking, Roosevelt pp. 262-63.

37. Perking, Roosevelt, p.263; Roosevelt, Public Papers, VII (Aug. 16, 1938), p.489.

38. Roosevelt, Public Papers, VII (Apr. 30, 1938), pp.333-34.

39. The New York Times, May 6, 7, 1938; Perking, Roosevelt, pp.263-64 (Perking makes an error in the date of Lister Hill's primary victory); Jonathan Grossman and James Anderson, interview with Clara Beyer, Nov, 5, 1965.

40. Record of Discussion of FLSA of 1938. V (U.S. Department of Labor), p. 873.

41. "Interview with Clara Beyer, No. 25, 1965; U.S. Record of Discussion of FLSA of 1938. V (U.S. Department of Labor), pp. 873, 915, 929.

42. Record of Discussion of FLSA of 1938. V (U.S. Department of Labor), p. 902.

43. Roosevelt, Public Papers, VI (May 24, 1937), pp. 214-16.

Chapter 2

Arguments For & Against Minimum Wage

Arguments Against

1. Minimum wages (MW) cut the hours and number of jobs available for low wage candidates & incumbents
2. MW causes inflation
3. MW erodes the buying power of middle and upper classes who don't receive raises
4. MW increase cost of business inputs
5. Some businesses that rely on MW workers would be forced into bankruptcy
6. New businesses that rely on MW workers would not open for business
7. Hurts smaller businesses
8. Displaces poorest & disadvantaged incumbents
9. MW increases cause depreciation of the U.S. dollar
10. Might result in exclusion of certain ethnic or gender groups
11. Might result in higher long-term unemployment for some
12. Slows growth of low skill jobs

13. MW is less effective at reducing poverty than other methods such as Earned Income Tax Credit
14. Causes migration of jobs to lower MW states and/or foreign countries
15. Discourages educational achievement due to enticing low skill workers to enter job market
16. Decreases overall employment participation
17. Redistributes wealth from upper class to the lowest class
18. When I eat at McDonalds, shop at Wal-Mart or call AT&T, most of the time I interact with incumbents who make MW. The cashier or representative, for all intents and purposes, is the face of the company. And given their relative experience, is that the best use of talent?

Arguments for Minimum Wage

1. Economic and social upward mobility is not as robust as originally thought so the MW boosts ability of low wage incumbents to rise in class
2. All businesses will see increased sales due to spending of money by many MW incumbents
3. In the U.S. economy jobs are created because of demand primarily from lower class and middle class members. The rich create business to capture lower class and middle class spending
4. Inflation due to MW is not nearly as severe as inflation caused by appreciation of the stock market. More inflation comes from the Dow Jones going from 6,443 in March 2009 to 17,068 in July 2014 than from MW going from $7.25 to $10.10
5. Business costs due to employee turnover is lower. It costs less to do hiring, training, and retaining employees because they stay with the company
6. More people are drawn into the labor market increasing labor participation rates even when adjusted for employment loses
7. Since more people are working, government transfer payments such as SSDI, SSI, SNAP and unemployment compensation are much lower

8. Morale is boosted among those receiving MW
9. Even if poverty is not reduced by a large amount, MW workers have an increased standard of living
10. Efficiency and automation is stimulated in many businesses
11. Removes low wage jobs forcing incumbents to develop and use higher order talents, skills, and abilities that otherwise would have been dormant
12. Reduced economic inequality
13. Broader distribution of all available hours for work so more people can have a decent job
14. Reduces black-market for illegal activities because more people will want to work
15. More incumbents feel valued and productive
16. Perhaps society in general will be more happy
17. Raising MW encourages more people to work.
18. A low MW encourages high employee turn-over costing business in recruitment & training
19. A low MW breeds less loyalty to one company
20. A low MW probably leads to lower quality results on the job
21. A low MW may lead to increased customer service complaints
22. A low MW encourages candidates to leave the workforce and collect government benefits

Point and Counter Point

Point: MW workers "think that money just appears out of thin air and that business owners can afford to pay them." **Counterpoint:** Many businesses can afford it. Cash stockpiled in most of the top 2000 businesses in America could be used to fund payrolls and not share-buybacks or outrageous executive paydays. Business has more cash now than at any other period of time. After all, when they off-shored production to cut costs where did the "savings" go? Obviously not to the middle and lower class.

Point: "If a business has to close because it can't afford to pay its workers, how beneficial really is this wage increase?" **Counterpoint:** Very few businesses could not afford to absorb slightly higher

MW. A typical McDonald's would need to increase the cost of a Big Mac by 10 cents or a typical value meal from $6.00 to $6.60 to cover a $10.10 per hour MW.

Point: "It's so annoying seeing lower income workers blaming rich people for their financial situation. The 1% are the people who make the jobs for them to work. Once you cripple the upper class, the lower class also falls." **Counterpoint:** Yes, people should take responsibility for their plot in life, but if only MW jobs are available what are they supposed to do? The 1% might make many of the jobs, but it is the sales and consumption of the middle and lower class that sustains these jobs. Without the spending of the middle and lower classes, there is no market. The entire structure of business, tax policy, and stock market is skewed in favor of the top 1%. They cannot be crippled because they create the rules by which the game is played. It is fool-hearty to expect that enriching the top 1% means the bottom 99% gets more crumbs.

Point: "There are people out there with college degrees who barely make $10.10 per hour, so why should a job that doesn't even require a degree make that much?" **Counterpoint:** The pay jobs get is dependent on how much revenue they bring in compared to input cost. Consider actors, musicians, athletes, and dancers. They get paid enormous sums not because they have a degree, possess a certification, or have very rare talent, but because the market they work in brings in lots of money. If people were paid by their value to society, surgeons, medical scientists, and teachers would be among the highest paid.

Point: "If MW goes up, the rest of us will make less." **Counterpoint:** The economy is not a zero sum game where advances by some mean less for others. There is plenty to go around because
wealth is created out of raw talent, inventions, and productivity, not by taking from the haves and giving to the have-nots.

Point: "For me, MW is $9.00 per hour and that is enough for anybody I know. For me at least, when I go out with my friends, I don't have to worry about money because MW is fairly high." **Counterpoint:**

Escaping Minimum Wage

It is a fallacy that most MW workers are teenagers with no financial obligations. The typical MW worker is older, with a high school diploma and supports herself. Many people in their prime working years are making MW jobs their career choice simply because there is nothing else in their community despite any level of education.

Point: "If the MW were raised to $10.10, inflation would occur."
Counterpoint: Many MW earners are stuck at MW and do not get raises. Inflation is going to happen whether or not MW is raised. They will be left behind. It is far more inflationary for the Dow Jones Industrial Average to go from 9,000 to 17,000 than any increase in MW could ever cause.

Point: "As workers become more productive, they command higher pay and move up their career ladder away from MW jobs."
Counterpoint: No, there is no clear career path for workers who work for minimum wage. With off-shoring jobs, mergers & acquisitions, and the dissolution of middle management and middle skill jobs, there is nowhere to go.

Point: "Raising the MW causes job loss and does not work as we think it should." **Counterpoint:** If MW hikes were detrimental, why do 19 states plus the District of Columbia have higher minimum wages than the Federally imposed $7.25 per hour? They probably want to stimulate the economy, bring in talent that would otherwise decay, and provide a strong incentive to work.

Point: "The notion that workers are trapped earning $7.25 per hour for much of their working lives is mistaken and ignores the primary value of MW jobs. Their importance lies not in making workers more productive so they can command higher pay in the future." **Counterpoint:** The company funding MW jobs does not care about employees' career development. They just want Tab A inserted into Slot B correctly, quickly, and cheaply. It is unfortunate but the incumbent is solely responsible for her career development.

Point: "MW jobs are stepping-stones to better jobs." **Counterpoint:** Turn-over in MW jobs is very high, often going above 150% in a given year with the average tenure of about 8 months. Those who work in MW jobs gain very few transferable skills that other, better-paying firms value. And if one stays in a MW job too long, her next employer may wonder why she has not taken better opportunities.

Point: "Firms paying MW will have to lay-off incumbents if MW is hiked." **Counterpoint:** Few incumbents would see this happen. A restaurant like McDonald's or a store like Family Dollar is already working with as few employees as possible. If MW were increased to $10.10, it would have more impact on new business ventures and not impact existing ones much. In either case, costs would be passed along to the consumer as it always is, but be assured its impact would be minimal despite what the opposition would have you believe.

Point: "The labor market works best under laizen-farre. It will determine fair wages without the involvement of the government." **Counterpoint:** The reason we have a MW is because business did take advantage of its employees. Exploitation of child labor, exploitation of adult labor, indiscriminant cutting of wages, and excessive hourly workweeks were the original founding causes behind MW. To be accurate, some firms did and will take advantage of its workers, and some did not and would not take advantage of its workers, but how can you make sure that the some who did, joined the all who did not without binding everyone to MW laws?

Point: "If a candidate does not want to work for MW, then do not take the job." **Counterpoint:** If only MW jobs are available, they will be filled because that is the only viable option.

Point: "Supporters of the MW intend it to lift low income families out of poverty." **Counterpoint:** No, this not its intent. MW exists to eliminate exploitation by the employer and create a floor to support America's non-unionized and unaffiliated workers. Lifting incumbents out of poverty is secondary to this.

Point: "MW jobs are where teenagers work part-time while in school." **Counterpoint:** True, but MW jobs are increasingly seen as out-right, permanent career choices for incumbents over age 25 because they can find no other work. The erosion of middle class jobs by conscious design by American Fortune 1000 companies is at play here.

Point: Boehner (2013), Speaker of the House, said, "When you raise the price of employment, guess what happens? You get less of it." **Counter-point:** A typical business employing large numbers of MW workers like Pizza Hut or Days Inn is already working with as few employees as possible. If they could do with one less server or housekeeper, then they would have already done so. Increasing pay and increasing numbers employed is the surest way to stimulate the economy, drive strength, and create prosperity for worker and employer.

Point: Supporters of the MW intend it to lift incumbents out of poverty. **Counter-point:** The original intent of the law was to prevent exploitation of workers who had little power against business owners. MW should lift incumbents to a point where they can live independently, and not be dependent on any governmental program.

Point: MW positions are typically learning wage positions. **Counter-point:** Yes they are, simply because an incumbent has to start somewhere. However, some choose to make it a deliberate career choice because it is convenient and they enjoy the work. Additionally, in many markets there really is not much else to do for a living.

Point: As workers become more productive they command higher pay and move up their career ladder. Two-thirds of MW workers earn a raise within a year. Raising the MW makes such entry-level positions less available, in effect sawing off the bottom rung of many workers' career ladders. **Counter-point:** Productivity has not dictated pay since the termination of stakeholder capitalism by American firms beginning in the 1970s and continuing to today. One-third of MW incumbents do not receive a raise in one year, and they get left further behind. The other two-thirds who do get raises get less than 15 cents per hour more, which is insufficient by any stretch. Raising the MW is likely to cut about 10% of total MW jobs while the remaining 3.2 million incumbents would see a significant raise. The effect of cutting off the career ladder at the first step is true for a few who are already marginally attached to the work-force. The gains of the great majority outweigh the losses of a few.

Point: Most MW workers are high school drop-outs. **Counter-point:** Over 72% of MW workers possess a high school diploma, some college, a bachelor degree or graduate degree.

Point: One of the central premises of economics is that "demand curves slope downwards" – when prices rise people buy less of a good or service. The same is true of labor. When wages rise employers hire fewer workers. **Counter-point:** This is not always the case. Consider gasoline. When prices rose, Americans drove less. But when prices went back down, they did not increase their consumption once again. Instead, they learned. They learned that a small hatchback is always better on their gasoline budget than a large SUV. Something similar happens with labor and business. Once a business adapts a certain business strategy concerning labor, they find to operate their business it takes X number of MW employees. When the price of labor goes up, they still operate with X MW employees because it takes that many to run the business. If the business could be run with fewer employees, then they would have already cut labor to that amount.

Point: Higher MW encourages employers to replace less-skilled workers with more productive employees. Given the choice between hiring an unskilled worker for $10.10 an hour and a worker with more experience for the same rate, companies will always choose the more experienced and productive employee. **Counter-point:** This simply is not true. If that were true, all candidates with experience and college degrees would have an unemployment rate of 0%. At the current MW rate of $7.25 or even the proposed rate of $10.10, business using MW labor is unlikely to draw candidates who have college degrees. The bottom rung of the career ladder stays where it is, and the floor it creates elevates and motivates those with and without high school diplomas to seek work. In short, higher skilled candidates will not work for MW even if it is $10.10. All that is left available to retail, hospitality, and personal service firms are the relatively less skilled regardless of productivity.

Point: As MW incumbents gain skill and experience, raising their productivity, they realize income gains. **Counter-point:** In the years after WWII, increases in productivity increased pay for everyone involved. This was called Stakeholder Capitalism. After 1970, increases in productivity lead to huge increases in pay for top executives, but left incumbents flat at best. The old idea that you get paid what you are worth does not always hold true. This change is called Shareholder Capitalism. Put another way, as given by the AFL-CIO, top executives in America's top 350 corporations had earnings 331X that of their average employee. That is, $11.7 million vs. $35,300. Do the top executives really earn all of that because of the value they bring to the company or do they simply take what they can since they make the rules?

Point: MW incumbents are lucky to have "any" job. **Counter-point:** When corporations say this, you can be sure they are taking advantage of them. In the sweat-shops of the turn-of-the century (19th to 20th), the incumbents were told this, and they accepted it because there was nothing else to do. Clearly the balance of power in work, wages, and opportunity has swung far to the extreme in favor of business owners and the rich. Perhaps, the time is ripe for a resurgence in labor unions.

Point: Technology has been the main force behind the long-term increases in income in the rich world (i.e., North America & Europe), not exploitation of the poor. **Counter-point:** Although this is technically true, it does not mean the poor (i.e., those working for MW) have reaped income gains over the same time, regardless of much increased productivity. Despite this, however, the standard of living has certainly increased for everyone over this time.

Point: As MW workers earn more, their government benefits decline, often in haphazard ways. Many MW workers would be better-off with a MW of $7.25 plus government benefits rather than an increase of MW to $10.10 plus reduced benefits. **Counter-point:** True, as MW incumbents earn more their benefits are reduced. There are many ways government benefits (SNAP, WIC, TANF, EITC, & Childcare Subsidies) could be restructured to provide a path to self-sufficiency without incurring losses of benefits as they try to better their lot in life. It is our responsibility to make honest work as beneficial and enticing as possible (not just financially) for both the benefit of the individual and society in general. And in doing so, we affirm the worth and dignity of all MW workers.

Discussion

When there is a large increase in MW, say, from $7.25 to $10.10, there should be a large increase in candidates that apply for MW work. But it is also likely that there will not be enough work to go around for all interested candidates. Thus, employers will have the freedom to be more selective in whom they hire for these jobs. And presumably, the least skilled and least experienced will not get a job, so unemployment will increase even as total employment will grow. Does an increase in MW price the least productive out of the job market? Many leading economists think it does, but I believe it may not.

I am not entirely sure you can compare commodities, such as wheat and gasoline to a "commodity" of labor. For wheat and gasoline, an artificial increase in price causes more to be produced along with lesser demand for it. When there is a surplus of wheat or gasoline, the government or investors may buy the excess. When there is a surplus of labor, candidates go unhired. However, the main difference between wheat and gasoline versus labor is that once labor is put to work it has organic growth, meaning that as more is produced more is demanded from what was produced. Labor that is hired at elevated prices, regardless if it is artificial or not, means those people have much more money to spend, which in turn produces more demand for the goods and services their labor produces. Excess wheat and gasoline do not have organic growth; their excess does not drive further demand.

Examining gasoline, we see that a higher price lowers demand and a lower price increases demand. But when the price of gasoline is high, people learn to drive more fuel-efficient cars, such that when gasoline prices decline there is no concomitant rise in consumption. People will have learned to make a new "normal." When the price of labor is high there is more demand for labor because there are now more people consuming. So when the price of labor declines, there is roughly the same demand. This occurs because a business has to operate with a certain number of employees, which is flexible only to a point. Inevitably, as prices for labor decline, some employees will drop-out of the workforce. This leaves the same amount of work to be done by fewer employees. This effect drives up productivity and pay for these incumbents, as long as this relationship is permitted to develop. Unfortunately, as we have seen, there has been a sharp disconnect between an increase in productivity and a corresponding increase in pay since the 1970s.

The Economist (Dec, 2013) said, "A minimum wage, providing it is not set too high, could thus boost pay with no ill effects on jobs …. America's federal minimum wage, at 38% of median income, is one of the rich world's lowest. Some studies find no harm to employment from federal or state minimum wage, others see a small one, but none finds any serious damage …. High minimum wages, however, particularly in rigid labour markets [unlike the U.S.A.], do appear to hit employment. France has the rich world's highest wage floor, at more than 60% of the median for adults and a far bigger fraction of typical wage for the young. This helps explain why France also has shockingly high rates of youth unemployment: 26% for 15-to-24-year-olds." If this line of thinking is valid, why is there such a big argument over raising pay for less than 5% of the workforce? In a word, politics.

Minimum wage laws affect workers in most low-paid fields of employment, such as hospitality (i.e., restaurants & lodging), personal services, and retail. Usually the law's effectiveness has been judged against its ability to lower poverty; but, recall that this function was not part of the original intent of FLSA of 1938. Yet, this function has gradually become the rationale de post facto of the law. This development is important because it is how the law is judged for efficacy today. The major problem with this approach is the fact that all of the organizations that are for or against MW laws have intense political, ideological, financial, emotional, and moral grounds for doing so. Often they emphasize research that supports only their particular point of view without considering the strength of the evidence opposite it. For example, Republicans tend to be against raising MW because their constituency desires cheap labor, whereas Democrats tend to be in favor of increasing MW because they desire the vote of the group who is positively affected by the law. Additionally, many non-government organizations, such as unions, political action committees, and businesses, large and small, have very narrow reasons why they support or reject MW law.

Unfortunately, it is difficult to uncover the greater good and potential failures of the MW law because more often than not it comes down to big money and political might instead of an exact science, despite hundreds of academic studies put forth. Minimum wage law can be successfully argued for or against using any particular point of view combined with selective use of available research. For this reason, MW research on the whole is, at best, unequivocal.

The push-back by business against MW can partly be explained by its unequal and relative impact on certain sectors of the economy. As we have noted, most MW laws affect hospitality, retail, and personal services much more often than the professional, management, and skilled, white-collar sectors. In effect, the former are penalized when the MW increases while the latter see little to no impact. This effect can be neutralized by certain alternatives to the MW law. Two such proposals are basic income and Earned Income Tax Credit.

The proposal of basic income is a transfer payment from the federal government that provides everyone, rich, middle class, or poor, with a sum of money that is sufficient to live on. The only qualification is citizenship. As far back as 1968, this scheme was proposed by more than 1,200 leading economists, but has been coldly received by Congress since then.

The Earned Income Tax Credit (EITC) is a program currently in place that pays low wage workers that have earned income from labor a sliding stipend to add to their yearly income. The EITC is popular in both parties. Presidents Carter, Reagan, H.W. Bush and Clinton have all expanded its use. In fact Ronald Reagan described the EITC as, "the best antipoverty, the best pro-family, the best job creation measure to come out of Congress." In many ways, the EITC is a superior method of providing low income workers with more income without penalizing their employers with a higher MW. Starkly, the EITC encourages lower income incumbents to work more, which of course, has all kinds of personal and societal gains whereas the basic income option doe not. Despite acceptance by both parties, its expansion has stalled temporarily, at least.

The data to follow comes from:

>www.IBISWorld.com/industry/default.aspx?indid=1980
>www.heritage.org/research/reports/2014/09/higher-fast-food-wages-higher-fast-food-prices

Examining the average fast food restaurant, we get:

Table 2-1: Selected Numbers for a Typical Fast Food Restaurant		
Measure	Per Store	Industry
Gross Revenue	$1,319,270	$199 B
Employees	24.4 FTE	3,686,048
Stores	-	150,841
Revenue per Employee	$53,987	$199 B
Revenue per Employee	$59,593	$220 B
Pay per Employee	$14,057	-
Pay per Employee	$19,582	-
Increase in Expense	$134,802	$21 B

Escaping Minimum Wage

Table: 2-2: Expenses of a typical fast-food restaurant

Expense	% of Total	Amount
Wages (1) $7.25	26%	$343,010
Wages (2) $10.10	36%	$477,813
Food & Paper	31%	$408,947
Depreciation	4%	$52,771
Marketing	3%	$39,578
Rent & Utility	9%	$118,734
All Other	24%	$316,625
Profit (before tax)	3%	$39,578
Total (1) $7.25	100%	$1,319,270
Total (2) $10.10	100%	$1,454,073

Table 2-3: Expenses per typical value meal

Expense	$6.00 Meal (1)	$6.60 Meal (2)
Wages	$1.56	$2.16
Food & Paper	$1.86	$1.86
Depreciation	$0.24	$0.24
Marketing	$0.18	$0.18
Rent & Utility	$0.54	$0.54
Other	$1.44	$1.44
Profit	$0.18	$0.18

So we see that increasing MW to $10.10 from $7.25 results in an increased expenditure of about 10%. The typical fast food restaurant would have to increase the typical value meal by about 60 cents. This move is likely to create a loss of a certain percentage of gross sales, but it is also likely that customers would absorb the increase in price. The customer may be willing to absorb this increase especially if it increases product quality, yields better customer service, and makes the transaction more enjoyable. And not to be overlooked, middle and lower class customers consume most fast food meals, which mirrors the incumbents producing the meal, so they purchase what they make. There are many other possible benefits. Consider these two: there would be a reduction in employee turn-over leading to lower costs for recruitment and training, and there would be an increase in the quality of labor received leading to better service, and perhaps, increased customer loyalty.

The argument that fast food restaurants would be forced to cut hours and eliminate jobs is largely unfounded. It is highly likely that most restaurants are already working with as few crew members as possible. And while some labor-saving automation might occur, it is likely that it would come over a long period of time and only reduce employment by a little. Fast food work requires a good deal of labor and what could be automated, already has been. Because of this, claims that reduced job opportunities would badly hurt less skilled workers are greatly exaggerated. McDonalds and other fast food restaurants do employ many teens in their first jobs, but from the demographic data shown in Chapter 1, the majority of incumbents are older and more experienced. They are taking these jobs more often as a deliberate career decision due to the flexibility and stability the work provides, and the somewhat remorseful fact that there is little else available to them.

Summary & Conclusions

Arguments for and against MW, often use selected statistics, only supporting what the person wants to emphasize. However, a careful evaluation using better weighting of the strengths and weaknesses is sorely needed. Many pundits cherry-pick certain statistics and then base their entire conclusion on them. The data shown here enables the reader to evaluate MW as both positive and negative. Yes, raising the MW will probably cost a limited number of jobs and it will increase input costs for operating a business that uses many MW workers. However, the jobs cut will be few because businesses using a lot of MW workers are already operating with the minimum of crew. If cuts do come, they will likely be seen in new ventures that do not yet exist. If the MW was raised from $7.25 to $10.10, overall costs to a typical fast food restaurant will increase by about 10%. The customer will likely see this as increased cost to eat there. While some customers will go elsewhere, it is likely they will accept the new pricing, especially if they get better service and know the additional cost is going to raise the wages of the people making their food.

"I can't imagine anything more worthwhile
than doing what I most love. And they pay me for it.
Edgar Winter

Chapter 3

Why You Can't Get Ahead

The present discussion on "Why You Can't Get Ahead" divides the issue into big picture effects and smaller, more individualistic effects. America currently has a decidedly more shareholder-capitalist structure as opposed to what was known as stakeholder capitalism. Stakeholder capitalism is responsible for the enrichment of everyone involved in the operation of a business. All members enjoyed success from top executive to common employee. Opposite this, under shareholder capitalism the rewards from success are funneled to select groups, namely the top executives, owners, and investors holding shares of the company. The differences between the two structures have implications for all constituents. Basically, America has lost its system of stakeholder capitalism. This event affects many things, such as pensions, unions, flow of money, trade, job security and the socio-economic class structure, among others.

To begin, let us examine labor unions and their status. Unions, in general, came about to protect the employee from exploitation, improve work environment, stabilize and increase wages, and provide for some measure of job security. When unions started, they were sorely needed to balance the way business owners treated their work force. And so, because of poor treatment, workers organized into unions and used collective bargaining to better their lot. This scheme proved successful for a time. Large gains in pay, security, and better working environments were achieved rather rapidly. And this enabled labor and management to share in their collective success. However, as time went along there was less and less need for unions, which also happened to dovetail with the increasing power of upper management and owners, who sought to weaken unions primarily on financial grounds. The results lead us to where we are today.

In the good times after World War II, 1954 saw the peak percentage of American workers that belonged to unions at 35%, whereas 1979 saw the peak membership in unions at 21.0 million incumbents, says Wikipedia.org (2014). Since then, both of these measures have fallen. Today, as given by the Bureau of Labor Statistics retrieved on 1/24/2014 union membership numbers stand at 14.5 million incumbents with a corresponding 11.3% of the total work force. Obviously, union power has diminished over the years; however, recently there has been a slight strengthening mainly due to more service workers and public employees joining and forming unions. Despite this, union influence is not what it once was, and that, is probably a bad thing. While the utility of unions can be debated with many positives and negatives, what is unequivocal is their positive effect on job security.

As unions have declined, at-will employment has seen a concomitant rise. Whether or not this is due to less need for unions or simply a result of stronger business ownership is difficult to ascertain. At-will employment is often stated as the right of either party to discontinue employment at any given time for almost any reason. At-will employment agreements make it easier to dissolve employee tenure for both employees who want to leave and employers who want to lay-off incumbents. The main advantage of this policy is that businesses are more confident in making hiring decisions since they have a way out if hard times occur. Incumbents benefit because they possess more mobility where they are free to take other, presumably better, opportunities. This is significant because incumbents will quit a job that is not fair, and then tell their friends that it is a poor opportunity, thus hurting the business' reputation. So what we have is a system where employers are unafraid to make bold hiring decisions and employees are empowered to leave unacceptable environments for whatever reason. This system is unlike what occurs in much of Europe (e.g., France) where it is very difficult or impossible to get rid of employees in a recession. This policy hampers business by depressing earnings, and ultimately, spills over into the entire economy, making recovery and growth very sluggish while artificially raising unemployment to high levels. After all, how many employees would be hired if a given company could not shed them when times got tough, or consider, how many incumbents would stay in a job where they were exploited? Clearly, having a rigid labor market is not productive. At-will employment makes the whole system more flexible, and perhaps better in America, at least.

Despite these positives, a policy of at-will-employment also means that by definition there is less job security. Incumbents who worry their tenure might be ended are not likely to make big financial or other important decisions. One effect that is gaining popularity is for high skill holders to make their services available on a case-by-case manner. This type of freelancing work results in contract work, such as a mechanical engineer being hired to complete one project. He would not be a member of the regular payroll, but would be paid more as an independent contractor since he would still have to factor in taxes and costs associated with obtaining new work. Time will tell if such arrangements are favorable. Whatever the particular arrangement, though, the important point to remember about at-will employment is that all of the risk of hiring, firing, and sustainability is borne by the worker, not the employer, and that is by design.

Employer-defined pensions have also changed as we have progressed further. It used to be quite common for firms to offer lifetime pensions to loyal, retiring employees. These pensions amounted to an annuity based on the worker's salary, such that well-seasoned employees received sizeable monthly payments. This arrangement worked fine until life expectancy grew, increasing the length of retirement years and the costs to the firm. Companies found that supporting previous employees in retirement was increasingly costly.

Pensions for rank-and-file retirees began to be eliminated starting in the 1970s. It accelerated through the 1980s and 1990s leaving few pensions in place today. They have been replaced with 401k, 403b, Roth IRA and traditional IRA accounts. Instead of a guaranteed monthly stipend, workers now take their chances in mutual funds, stocks and bonds in the stock market. This development is not a problem in a secular bull market, but in severe downturns sizeable chunks of retirement savings can be lost. If an incumbent is not savvy enough to understand this and other risks, such as when to sell and get out of the stock market as retirement approaches, they could face an unfortunate retirement spent waiting on Social Security checks, cutting coupons, and working part-time to make ends meet. On the other hand, investing long-term in the stock market is nearly guaranteed to create more savings than would be had with a company pension. The important take away to remember about the demise of pensions and the rise of 401ks is that all of the risk is borne by the employee, and that is by design.

International trade is the next area that changed the 20th century. American Fortune 500 companies found they could transfer manufacturing to emerging markets like China, Brazil, India, and Mexico to realize savings on both labor costs and taxes. Foreign workers in these areas were very willing to work for these lowered wages that Americans would never accept. These multinational companies found that people would work not for what they were worth, but instead would work for what they were offered and willing to accept. Lou Dobbs said, "The power of big business over our national life has never been greater. Never have there been fewer business leaders willing to commit to the national interest over selfish interest, to the good of the country over that of the companies they lead. And the indifference of those business leaders to our long term national welfare is nowhere more evident than in the exporting of American jobs to cheap overseas labor markets." For example, NAFTA (North American Free Trade Agreement) transformed a relatively manageable trade deficit with our neighbors into a full-blown problem. While U.S. exports to Mexico and Canada have increased by 57%, imports have risen 96%. As a result, the U.S. trade deficit with these two countries has ballooned from $9 Billion in 1993 to $87 Billion last year [2003] – and it's only getting worse." Note that this was over

10 years ago. In 2012, U.S. trade with Canada is even and with Mexico it stands at a $50 Billion deficit. Progress, perhaps, but painfully slow. Make absolutely no mistake about it; higher productivity, more efficiency, and greater competitiveness are really just code words for cheaper, cheaper, and cheaper.

Entire U.S. industries were exported this way. Consider, ceramics, steel, textiles, electronics, and furniture to name a few. And so, the American worker loses his job to a Chinese worker because the latter is willing to work for $10 per day. The American worker collects his unemployment check, not because he wants to, but because he has to. The jobs are gone; there is nothing else for him. On the other hand, at least he can afford to buy the inexpensive Chinese trinkets that are massively imported. As it is, low prices for inferior junk have been exchanged for good-paying, middle class American jobs. What is really interesting to ponder is to try and figure out where all the cost savings from off-shoring production of, say, a shirt went since the price of the shirt remained the same. Of course, the executives and shareholders of these off-shored businesses make evermore plump profits, but to what end. The important thing to take away from open, free trade and the American worker is that he loses his job, which paid well, so the now multinational company can draw hefty profits by selling and importing cheap versions of what the American worker used to make. Here again we see that the risk is off-loaded from the company on to the backs of the American employee and consumer.

Off-shoring, automation, and merger/acquisition are catching up with us. We are running out of good middle class jobs and middle class consumers that drive demand for goods and services. Robert Reich (2010), Secretary of Labor under President Clinton, said, "After three decades of flat wages during which almost all the gains of growth have gone to the very top, the middle class no longer has the buying power to keep the economy going." Three measures bear this out: First, from *Forbes* (2/16/2014) the middle 60% of the wage distribution (20th to 80th percentile) owned 53% of the total wealth pie in 1970, by 2012 it dropped to just 45%. Second, Pew Research (2/16/2014) says the median income within the middle class (not the overall median, but just in the middle class) has dropped 10%. And third, the FiscalTimes.com

(4/4/2013) reports that 47.8 million people receive an average of $133 in monthly food stamps (SNAP). In April 2013, the FiscalTimes.com reported, "A recovering economy should expand the workforce and reduce reliance on safety-net programs. Instead we see the opposite." Food Stamps (SNAP) has exploded in recent years. See Table 3:1.

Table: 3-1: Number on Food Stamps with Average Award

Year	Millions	Average
2013	47.6	$133
2007	26.3	$96
2000	17.2	$73
1990	22.0	$59
1979	17.6	$31
1970	4.0	$11

Clearly, wealth has evaporated for many middle class incumbents to the extent that millions have landed in poverty.

All of the statistics above are correct as far as they go. Most measures largely ignore the greatly increased quality and variety of goods and services available today, as compared to any point in the past. This means that even if wages do not grow, everyone still sees increases in standard of living. The Bureau of Labor Statistics (bls.gov) reports that average wages do not account for untaxed, fringe benefits, such as healthcare insurance, pensions, and paid leave. These are very significant comprising an extra 31% of overall compensation. Again, that boosts quality of life. *The Wall Street Journal* (2013) says the average wage incorporates large numbers of women and immigrants who began to be employed during the previous 40 years. This has the effect of skewing the distribution far towards the lower wage levels. Since most candidates enter the labor force at wages much lower than the average, this group is huge and growing, and responsible for holding down growth of average wages. Experienced incumbents quickly moved up the wage scale over this same period of time, and their numbers are increasing today, but there are still many fewer of them in comparison to new labor market candidates. And finally according to *The Wall Street Journal*, the amount consumers spend on the basic necessities has dropped. In 1950, consumers spent 53% of their disposable income on home, utilities, food, automobiles, clothing, shoes, furnishings, and electronic equipment. By 1970 it was 44%, and dropped further to 32% in 2013. All of this means that: quality of life increased, wages remained steady, millions of workers were added to the work force, incumbents moved up in pay, and consumers pay less of their disposable income on necessities. But all of this also means that: middle class wealth is less in absolute numbers, 1 in 5 Americans receive food assistance, and spending by the middle class is lower in absolute numbers.

The rich do not create most jobs, as they would have you believe. Instead it is demand from the middle class who has discretionary income to spend. The lower class also participates but their extra money is limited even though their numbers are large. The upper class spends a lot, but by greatly fewer numbers. After all, how many refrigerators does Warren Buffett need? And so right or wrong, we have progressed from a production economy to a consumer economy.

The loss of middle class jobs has to eventually exact a cost to our economy through lower profits if not outright losses. We reap as we have sown. The important point to take away is that once again risk is off-loaded from business to the American employee and consumer, and all that you have to do to see this effect is follow the trail of money. That is, from the middle and lower classes to the upper class.

Over the course of the last decade, the Cleveland Federal Reserve Bank reports the poverty rate in the U.S. rose from 11.3% to 15.0%. From a geographic perspective, this increase has been widespread with 49 of 50 states seeing increases in poverty. Clearly, the rise in poverty is linked closely to economic conditions, with many families and individuals realizing declining incomes during the Great Recession. The U.S. Census Bureau (2010) defines the poverty threshold to be $22,113 for a family of four with two children. Poverty level is defined as the amount needed to provide food, clothing, and shelter for healthful living. The figure cited above represents a 32% premium above the MW of $15,080.

What this means is that a father working full-time at MW would not be able to fully support his family. He needs to earn $10.63 per hour instead of $7.25 per hour. MW jobs were fine when incumbents were not expected to make it a career. Twenty years ago teenagers worked these jobs and they had few financial obligations, so it was not a problem. Today people over age 25 with families work these jobs as deliberate career choices simply because there is little else to pick from. Americans work hard and are very productive, but this raw effort and increase in productivity is no longer justly rewarded. This occurs as big business claims foreigners can save them money because of increased productivity. Is that not hypocritical? What they really mean is that Americans are not willing to work for $10 per day as they do in India and China. Table 3-1 Median Income is provided for reference.

Table 3-2: Median Income by Country		
Country	U.S. Dollars	Rank
Luxembourg	$37,200	1
Norway	$33,900	2
Switzerland	$33,700	3
United States	$30,900	4
Australia	$30,100	5
Canada	$28,400	7
Germany	$24,600	12
France	$24,200	15
United Kingdom	$21,500	19
Japan	$20,000	22
Mexico	$4,500	35

Escaping Minimum Wage

According to the World Values Survey, "while 60% of Europeans say they think, "the poor are trapped in poverty," only 29% of Americans think so. Instead 60% of Americans think, "the poor are lazy," compared with just 26% of Europeans." This finding shows how Americans and Europeans are different. The Europeans have their aristocracies and rigid class systems whereas Americans are united in the belief that everyone with their given talents and persistent, hard work can make it to the top. Benjamin Friedman writing in *The Atlantic* (7-8/2014) emphasizes this point by saying, "As Tocqueville [the French political philosopher] observed after visiting the new republic [America], the widespread perception that anyone can get ahead creates a presumption that everyone has an obligation to at least try." These two statements starkly point out that Americans do not expect to be trapped in poverty as our European peers might be, and that in America everyone is expected to contribute and pull his/her own weight. The former of these statements may be less accurate than we would like, yet it is what we expect even if it is not true. The latter one, of course, is firmly ground-into every kid from Kindergarten onward to the point that as adult workers they find it unpatriotic to use all of their paid vacation days.

Tocqueville goes on to say, "Among a democratic people [like Americans], where there is no hereditary wealth, every man works to earn a living ... Labor is held in honor; the prejudice is not against but in its favor." Americans believe all men are created equal, and as such, are only held back by their desire to work hard. So we are to conclude that inequality in societal standing, especially when determined by wealth, is due to a man's sloth. In fact, Tocqueville goes on to explicitly cite inequality as being the incentive for the poor to become rich. The lesson learned is work hard and you will get rich.

This entire line of thinking is fine until someone upsets the applecart. Economic inequality in America is only palatable if the poor and middle classes think they can make it to the top. The poor and middle classes must believe that through hard work alone, they too can become wealthy and have their wants satisfied. Whether or not they actually can is not nearly as important as perpetuating the illusion that it is a possibility. Once the covenant is broken, however, repairing the damage is likely to be a bloody mess. Tocqueville laments, "But one also finds in the human heart a deprived taste for equality, which impels the weak to want to bring the strong down to their level, and which reduces men to preferring equality in servitude to inequality in freedom."

And so we will soon face the tipping point, where the poor and middle classes learn the truth, and fortunately for us, the truth has yet to be cast in stone. We have time to change course. The rich and power elite, who have surely reaped the benefits of money and connection, must find ways to empower and employ an expanding middle class, and energize, encourage, and help the poor achieve upward mobility on their terms. A failure here means the poor and middle classes will unite to remove the upper class from power. Then, they will take back what was taken from them, even though it was taken from them under cloak of law. After all, it is the rich and powerful who write such laws for their benefit.

"Everyone has been made for some particular work,
and the desire for that work has been put in every heart."
Rumi

Reasons why you cannot get ahead are discussed below.

1. Lack of a marketable skill: Perhaps, you have no training beyond high school or your skills are considered obsolete. Even high school graduates possess marketable skills, such as reading, writing, mathematics, computing, and presenting. A community college often has programs that are quick and in demand in your particular area. Consider, licensed practical nursing, registered nursing, welding, early childhood education, landscaping, social services, computerized bookkeeping, or an associate of arts for transfer to a four year college or university.

2. Lack of valued experience: If you are in school, try to get an internship or cooperative opportunity in a local business. Do not forget you can always volunteer as an intern to open doors that were previously shut. It is no longer acceptable to graduate from high school or college without doing some experiential work. A degree with no experience is not a good way to start your career.

3. Poor Planning: If you cannot plan what you really want to do, then you will never make it beyond step one. Planning forces you to predict what the future (i.e., your future) may hold. Try to project yourself into the future by starting every major activity with the end in mind. If you know where you want to be in two years, you are much more likely to make it. If you are deciding on a major in college, pretend you already have the degree and relevant experience and do a job search. This will help you judge whether or not the degree will be employable where you want to live.

4. Inability to focus: Often those who do not focus well, do not understand the value of what they are doing. Redouble your efforts in understanding the why behind what you want to do. The what to do should come readily after that. Take it in small chunks, so you can process it all. Divide and conquer, the saying goes.

5. Fatalistic attitude: Although it may seem that nothing you do makes a significant difference, in reality you have much more decision-making

power than you give yourself credit for. Talk with others about your plan and why you think it can be achieved. Nothing happens unless you make it happen. Think, if it is to be, it is up to me. Thomas Jefferson said, "Nothing can stop the man with the right mental attitude from achieving his goal; nothing on Earth can help the man with the wrong mental attitude."

6. Attitude of entitlement: The world owes you nothing. To get what you want you must give something of value in exchange for it. This fact is true in every transaction. For example, suppose you are a dishwasher. The restaurant values clean dishes more than the money that they pay you. You, on the other hand, value the money more than the time spent washing dishes. In this exchange, each party gets what it values more, and both are happy with the negotiation. Lou Holtz, the former football coach at Notre Dame, said, "Ability is what you are capable of doing. Motivation determines what you do. Attitude determines how well you do it."

7. Lack of savings: "I have never been unhappy relying on money that I have saved." A man does not know what the day may bring, so it is best to prepare for the most likely problems. If you cannot save, then you will never get ahead. You will be unable to take advantage of the opportunity when it comes, and you will feel foolish.

8. Discrimination: Whether you are a minority, a woman, disabled, older than 40, or belong to another protected class, you can almost count on being discriminated against at some point in your life. The trick is to recognize it and know that it is their problem not yours. It probably was not a very good opportunity anyhow. Scott Hamilton said, "The only disability in life is a bad attitude."

9. Psychopathology: Perhaps you suffer from anxiety, depression, alcoholism, or drug use. If you truly desire to change your life, visit a counselor, doctor, therapist, or clergy member to take positive steps. Even if you cannot fully overcome your particular problem, it can usually be minimized with treatment. All problems have very promising treat-

ments if you will try them. Do not lose hope. Remember you are not alone in your suffering.

10. Family pressures: Children, sick spouses, and forgetful parents might be causing you stress. If it is, find someone to talk to so you can decompress. Then, enlist someone else who may fill in for you from time to time. Do the same for them and you both reap benefits.

11. No passion in what you are doing: A job is a long string of completing tasks. When you do not enjoy the process of completing these tasks, it does not matter what the pay is. You will not find it enjoyable or meaningful. Find something you love (i.e., the actual activities) and then it really is not like work. Consider, what would you do for free? Would you, perhaps, announce basketball games, become a pilot, or become a commercial fisherman? Find it, then do it. It was Charles Schwab, who said, "The man who does not work for the love of work, but only for money is not likely to make money nor find much fun in life."

12. Lack of hard work: Hard work alone is never enough. Those in MW jobs work very hard. The stereotype that the poor do not work hard is not accurate. Often they work harder than most middle managers even if it is because of physical labor. Hard work will open doors, but if that is all you offer, you will be disappointed. It takes hard work plus a passion for something where you can become one of the best at it. Olympian, Bruce Jenner claims, "I learned that the only way you are going to get anywhere in life is to work hard at it. Whether you are a musician, a writer, an athlete, or a businessman, there is no getting around it. If you do, you will win. If you do not, you will not." He also rightly assumes we have the talent to be a musician, writer, athlete, or businessman. Once you uncover a talent, begin your hard work on it so you can become the best at it.

13. Undeveloped talent: Talent alone is never enough. Everyone has talent. It also takes hard work, persistence, passion, and perhaps, someone to help you along the way. Be the person who helps others find their talent, and you might just find yours. "Finding an outlet for your best

15. Lack of opportunity: There is no such thing as no opportunity. Just look around or talk to your peers; it will show itself soon enough. "Jumping at several small opportunities may get us there more quickly than waiting for one big one to come along," espoused Hugh Allen. If you show that you are responsible with a little, you will soon be trusted with a lot. Sun Tzu's classic, ages-old strategy says, "Opportunities multiply as they are seized." Begin with the right ingredients, take a risk, work hard and soon enough the path will be rendered easy.

16. Lack of courage: Whether you start in poverty, come from a broken family, have experienced abuse or neglect, live in the poor part of town, have some sort of disability, or have any number of seemingly insurmountable circumstances, it is not about what has happened that matters, but instead, it is all about what you are going to do now. Those things pale in importance when compared to your resolve to make a plan and see it through. At any time, all you have to do is believe you can, and sure enough with courage and persistence, you will.

Notes
Wikipedia.org (retrieved 11/02/2014).
    En.wikipedia.org/wiki/Labor_unions_in_the_United_States

Online.wsj.com/news/articles/
SB10001424127887323468604578249723138161566

Forbes.com/sites/joelkotkin/2014/02/16/the-u-s-middle-class-is-turning-proletarian/

Fiscaltimes.com/Columns/2013/04/04/a-food-stamp-recovery-is-the-new-normal#page1

Ustr.gov/countries-regions/Americas/Canada

Ustr.gov/countries-regions/Americas/Mexico

Fns.usda.gov/sites/default/files/pd/SNAPsummary.pdf

Chapter 4

Poverty

The reasons why someone remains in poverty and works for minimum wage as a career choice are never just financial. Instead it includes an outlook set on scarcity, which is the perspective that abundance is not for them. It also includes a lack of diverse, accessible resources and a dependence on others, especially the government. They often view the prevailing labor market structure and function as being against them, not to help them. Ruby Payne (1996) in *A Framework for Understanding Poverty* says, "... a working definition of poverty is the extent to which an individual does without resources." She goes on to define resources as being "financial, emotional, mental, spiritual, physical, relationships and role models, external support systems, and knowledge of hidden rules." In her second paragraph she claims (which shows the value of her volume) that, "Typically, poverty is thought of in terms of financial resources only. However, the reality is that financial resources, while extremely important, do not explain the differences in the success with which individuals leave poverty nor the reasons that many stay in poverty. The ability to leave poverty is more dependent upon other resources than it is upon financial resources." So how can resources other than financial ones go further to explain why most of America's poor remain so?

It's More than Financial

This question is difficult to answer because it appears poverty and reliance on minimum wage-type jobs cannot be reduced to just numbers in a bank account. One anecdotal example that helps crystallize why most remain poor and others do not is given in the observation that many who win millions of dollars in the lottery are completely broke in a few short years. It is not a lack of money (i.e., the financial), but a lack of an abundance mindset that holds them down.

Another example is found in wealth redistribution. Frankly, it is occurring but without success. If we were to take all the money from CEOs, large companies, and everyone else with substantial funds and redistribute it to the bottom 99% of the wage scale, we would most likely see in a short time that all the money would migrate back to its original owners. Herein we discover the cause of poverty and reliance on minimum wage jobs is most certainly not only about "bucks" and "quid," even though many who set policy decisions think it is.

Adoption of Fatalism

Ms. Payne goes on to say, "In poverty, the clear understanding is that one will never get ahead, so when extra money is available, it is either shared or immediately spent." If one thinks he will never get ahead, he is right, he never will. Fatalism robs his motivation, and with it his resolve. The first thing to do is believe a life above poverty and minimum wages is possible. Without a belief that it is possible, he never makes plans that will pay off. Many fail to see any improved possibilities because they associate with others who have the same fatalistic view. Therefore, they never see anyone progress out of financial bondage. To begin a journey out of minimum wage and poverty, one must think it possible. That is, the thought must occur to him and resonate in him.

Role of Language

Ms. Payne cites Montano-Harmon (1991) who reveals that students who come from poverty do not have access to formal register at home. Formal register is standardized English that has recognized sentence syntax, appropriate word choice, and complete thoughts. It is the approved register, or language, of the middle class. It is the language of commerce, all schooling (i.e., K-12 & Higher Education), standardized tests (e.g., ACT, SAT & Civil Service Exams), and middle-income jobs. Without it, communication, etiquette, and standards can be difficult to understand. Since many students from poverty do not know how to use formal register and instead rely on casual register that they use with friends, they often remain in poverty in later life. This fact is especially detrimental because they may have the necessary desire and nuanced talent to be successful, but never get the chance because of their poor grammar and diction. Not only does it hamper their scores on standardized tests, but it also excludes them when interviewing for well-paying jobs that could go a long way in lifting them up. One of the reasons why a college degree is considered the passport to the middle class is that it "certifies" a graduate as being sufficiently educated in formal register, among many other outcomes.

Because of this and a confluence of other factors, those in poverty strongly tend to end up in minimum wage jobs where written and verbal communication is not viewed or used at a premium. They rely on casual register at home and with peers despite needing to use it at school. They have no role models who work in middle class jobs. And because of this, they have no inkling of what constitutes someone's day at work in a middle class, middle skill job. Conversely, middle class students are immersed in formal register at home, in all schooling, and by significant role models. This familiarity with formal register makes it easy for them to aspire to middle class professions because they already "know the ropes."

Job Elimination & Simplification

All that those in poverty have access to (i.e., their resources) delivers them to low skill, lower class, minimum wage jobs. It used to be that with time and experience most minimum wage jobs led to middle class jobs. However now, with more frequency, minimum wage jobs are turning into permanent career choices. Prior to the 2000s, minimum wage jobs acted as stepping-stones to middle class jobs. This event is happening less and less because of two main reasons, the "dumbing-down" of minimum wage jobs and the outright elimination of middle class jobs.

First, minimum wage jobs have been "dumbed-down," so that the most inexperienced (i.e., usually from the lower class) can make a valued contribution. Job duties have been reduced to very rudimentary tasks. For example, minimum wage jobs in the hospitality sector are limited in scope. They have been standardized, and in doing so, demand only limited thinking and responsibility. These types of jobs consist of repetitive, routine tasks. Complex skills are not taught and are not valued. Consequently, an incumbent never develops higher abilities, and more importantly, never acquires complex, transferable skills used in middle class employment opportunities.

Second, corporate America has eliminated many middle income jobs through the flattening of hierarchies, pushing more jobs to emerging markets that demand less pay, and reducing redundancy of positions when merging with and acquiring other firms. The results of hundreds of decisions like these have shaped America's labor market. College graduates have fewer good choices for jobs in the middle of the pay scale. They are increasingly being underemployed in minimum wage-type jobs, thus displacing candidates and incumbents who do not possess desirable education, valued experience, and other important traits. This is precisely why we have 15,000 parking lot attendants and 40,000 building cleaners who have bachelor degrees. There simply are not enough middle class jobs for all college graduates. When they enter the workforce after school, they take jobs previously held by high school graduates, and so everyone is bumped down one notch.

Values Not Shared

Poor people, the middle class, and the wealthy all value different things. According to Ms. Payne she says, "... the bottom-line [i.e., what is important] in generational poverty is entertainment and relationships. In middle class, the criteria against which most decisions are made relate to work and achievement. In wealth, it is the ramifications of the financial, social, and political connections that have weight." Naturally, whatever is valued, then that is what is acquired. It is not wrong to value any of these outcomes over any other, as long as that is what you want. The problem comes when one wants to move up socio-economically, but cannot because of what they value. "The key point is that hidden rules govern so much of our immediate assessment of an individual and his/her capabilities. These are often the factors that keep an individual from moving upward in a career – or even getting the position in the first place," says Ms. Payne. In this sense, their freedom is limited. The opportunity is unavailable.

Table: 4-1: What is Valued by Economic Status			
	Poverty	Middle Class	Rich
Possessions	People	Things	One-of-kind objects
Money	Spend	Manage	Conserve & Invest
Time	Present	Future	Traditions
Education	Abstract	Crucial	Maintains Connections
Driving Force	Survival	Work	Connections
Language	Casual	Formal	Formal for Networking
Destiny	Fate	Choice	Tradition
World View	Local	National	International

Traits Of Survival that Hold You Down

An interesting summary of poverty comes from Oscar Lewis in the *Four Horsemen,* "The economic traits which are most characteristic of the culture of poverty include the constant struggle for survival, unemployment and underemployment, low wages, a miscellany of unskilled occupations, child labor, the absence of savings, a chronic shortage of cash, the absence of food reserves in the home, the pattern of frequent buying of small quantities of food many times a day as the need arises, the pawning of personal goods, borrowing from local money lenders at usurious interest rates, spontaneous informal credit devices (tandas) organized by neighbors, and the use of second-hand clothing and furniture." These traits perpetuate poverty even as it enables their survival.

Middle Class Job Loss

Rana Foroohar writing in *Time* (2/10/2014) said, "The forces of globalization and technology tend to wipe out middle income jobs and favor those at the very top of the socio-economic ladder." She cites a current McKinsey Global Institute study that found 230 million white-collar jobs, representing about $9 Trillion in income will be transformed or eliminated by computers over the next decade [by 2024]. Clearly change is coming and if we are not careful lots of people will be left behind to struggle and toil in work they neither chose nor are prepared for. It seems we have a problem in finding some work to do for a good middle class existence.

Lou Dobbs (2004) in *Exporting America* says we are now as of 2004 witnessing the exportation of high-value jobs in information technology, financial services, law, and engineering to low cost labor markets all over the globe. He goes on to state that American workers are the most productive in the world. Yet, that does not seem to matter. "With the importation of a Trillion dollars of foreign-produced goods, we lose a Trillion dollars of the U.S. consumer market. And we have no way to make it up, because there is no foreign market large enough to replace that Trillion dollars." All of this comes to a head where, "The result of the importation of foreign manufactured goods is to dampen job creation, further erode our manufacturing base, widen our trade deficit, and worsen our position as debtor nation to the world," says Dobbs. Furthermore, "Corporate America is not exporting American jobs over seas to win access to foreign markets, but to take advantage of cheap foreign labor." After which, these corporations import the products that had just previously been manufactured here. Dobbs goes on to say, "When high wage manufacturing jobs are replaced with service sector jobs that pay at least 23% less, the downward pressure on the wages of Americans is accelerated." In essence, we are trading $25 an hour jobs in manufacturing for $12 an hour jobs in servicing, so we can afford to shop for cheap imports at Wal-Mart and Dollar General.

If America does not protect and expand on middle income, middle wage, middle class jobs, we risk becoming a nation of haves and have-nots with nothing in the middle. The reason global trade and technology favor those in the top 10% is because they are the ones who determine new policy, new law, and own businesses of all sorts. They have and will continue to set up the system for their benefit first. The way to a just society is not to give the very rich more so there will be more crumbs for everyone else. Quite the opposite is true. Empowering the poor with eroding more. In other words, a lot of the wealth in the stock market evaporates in recessions, but quickly resumes its upward trend once business sheds excess workers and resets itself for future profits. Simultaneously, middle class and lower class earnings decline rapidly in a recession due to job loss and stay lower because they are rehired at lower wages. So in a recovery, business and the rich are set up to do better, while the middle class and lower class are left with stagnant earnings on their labor, which of course, is where they get almost all of their income.

There are only eight ways to change income distribution:
1. Rich earn more as the rest earns the same.
2. Rich earn the same while the rest earns less.
3. Rich earn more as rest earns less.
4. Rich earn much more while the rest earns more.
5. Rich earn the same while rest earns more.
6. Rich earn less while rest earns the same.
7. Rich earn less while rest earns more.
8. Rich earn more as rest earns much more.

Of these, 1, 2, and 3 remind us of the robber-barons in the latter part of the 1800s and early part of the 1900s. Points 5, 6, and 7 happen rarely, if at all. Only points 4 and 8 describe a social structure that is fair and equitable.

Income inequality measures differences in incomes, not necessarily of opportunities. It focuses on societal welfare, which depends on variables such as consumption of goods and services, leisure and recreation, health and well-being, and public goods. It seems that income alone is not the only determinant of a good quality of life. The Heritage Foundation likes to report how much the poor have, like a home, two cars, air conditioning, two televisions, the internet and the like. Despite these gains in quality of life, there is still a great divide between the rich and the middle class and lower class in terms of power, freedom and security.

Education's Limits

Perhaps, education is the answer. Jacobson and Occhino claim, "Most of the rise in income inequality since 1980 has been attributed to an increase in the returns to education and in the wage differential between high skilled and low skilled labor." K-12 and higher education has its limits, though. After all, what good is a shiny-new, freshly-minted degree if business and industry has no job for the graduate. Just because a school offers training in a particular area and just because students play by the rules and study diligently for an average of five years, does not mean there are actual jobs waiting for them when they finish. There is a definite disconnect between what American business needs, wants, and can employ and what American education turns out in quality and quantity. It seems we have been sold a faulty bill of goods. And to be frank, education helps, but it mostly helps the few, who would have succeeded anyhow.

"Over time, the marginal productivity of high skilled workers has increased relative to low skilled workers, which has driven the demand for their labor higher and raised their relative compensation. As a result of this change, labor income became less evenly distributed and more concentrated at the top," say Jacobson and Occhino. In other words, we are to conclude that high skilled workers get paid more than low skilled workers because they are more productive, and thus more valued on the job. Starkly, the labor market pays its workers what it has to, not what they are worth, but what they are willing to accept (i.e., forced to accept). Do not those in social service, hospitality, the military, and education make worthwhile contributions often way beyond what those in professional sport, law, and corporate governance contribute? Unfortunately, there is little correlation between the hard work, intelligence, and real value one gives of him/herself and the money he/she is paid. Consider for a moment where American society and the economy would be without the extraordinary contributions of social workers, chefs, soldiers, and elementary school teachers. Eliminate those and we have no society to waste away at basketball games, sue for ill-gotten gain, or blame for insider trading.

Where to Now

If we are to believe Ms. Payne's conclusions about poverty, that factors other than financial ones cause and keep people in poverty, then it seems society has been focused on the wrong parameters. Throwing more and more money at a problem rarely solves it, especially when discussing non-financial causes. In this same vein, giving money to the poor is not the answer, yet that is all we seem to do. Perhaps, we need to concentrate as a society on creating a socio-economic structure where everyone can contribute where she is, with what she has, and at the class level she is most comfortable. Success does not have to look like what the rich have. Taking someone from poverty and elevating him to the upper class through money alone is probably not going to be the most effective use of limited resources. People seek people like themselves, and that should not be ignored. Who is to say that to be successful you have to go to college or adopt the values of the rich, and in the process shed your way of life and values, even if it is without a full complement of resources?

"Far and away the best prize that life has to offer is the chance to work hard at work worth doing."
Theodore Roosevelt

Escaping Minimum Wage

"You never know how strong you are
until being strong is the only thing you have."
Bob Marley

Chapter 5

Inventory of Resources

Consistent with Ruby Payne's idea that poverty is the extent to which one does without resources, below is an inventory that narrows what these resources are for you. The categories of resources are: financial, emotional, physical, mental, spiritual, support system, personal relationships, role models and knowledge of hidden rules for your socio-economic class. Each of these has its own repertoire of knowledge, skill, and ability. This list is provided to help you reveal all of the supports and resources you have available to you. It also let's you see where you could use extra support.

Financial: Circled _____ out of 61.
    Work Income
        Full-time Work
        Part-time Work
        Seasonal Work
        Sales Commission
        Temporary Work
        Union Membership
        Contract Assignment

Escaping Minimum Wage

Passive Income
- Interest
- Dividends
- Government Bonds
- Corporate Bond
- Common Stock
- Annuity
- Mutual Fund
- Collectibles
- Life Insurance
- Money Market Fund
- Precious Metals
- Real Estate Investment Trust
- Physical Real Estate
- Certificate of Deposit
- Municipal Bonds

Government Benefits
- Supplemental Nutrition Assistance Program
- Social Security
- Supplemental Security Income
- Social Security Disability
- Temporary Assistance to Needy Families
- Unemployment Compensation
- Worker's Compensation
- Earned Income Tax Credit
- Federal, State, Local Tax Refund
- Childcare Subsidy
- Heating & Cooling Assistance
- Medicare
- Medicaid

Other Income
- Alimony
- Child Support
- Roth & Traditional IRA

Escaping Minimum Wage

    Coverdell IRA
    529 College Savings

Student Income
    Work Study
    Pell Grant
    State Educational Grant
    Scholarships
    Stafford Student Loans
    Parent Student Loans
    Other Student Loans

All Other Forms of Income
    401k & 403b Plans
    Healthcare Savings Account
    Cafeteria Healthcare Plans
    Cash
    Checking
    Home Equity Loan
    Home Equity Line of Credit
    Garage Sales
    Ebay
    Craig's List
    Pawn Shop
    Recycling
    Gambling & Lottcry
    Blood, Plasma, Semen, Egg Stipends

Emotional Resources: Circled _____ out of 31.
    Control of Anxiety
    Stamina
    Perseverance
    Persistence
    Hope
    Optimism
    Control of Pessimism

Happiness
Empathy
Stability
Lack of Boredom
Understanding
Desire to Change
Control over Impulsivity
Resilience
Resolve
Motivation
Positive Attitude
Love
Caring
Friendship
Satisfaction
Control over Anger
Limit Sadness
Limit Depression
Readiness to Change
Lack of Hatred
Desire to Maintain
Control over Indecision
Lack of Rashness
Control over Irritability

Mental Resources: Circled _____ out of 24.
    Ability to Read
    Ability to Write
    Ability to Compute
    Ability to Speak
    Ability to Listen
    Memory
    Logic
    Possess Insight
    Estimate Time
    Spatial Awareness

Escaping Minimum Wage

Ability to Analyze
Ability to Employ Rationality
Ability to Use Computers
Integrity of Thought to Action
Ability to Compare & Contrast
Making Judgments
Ability to Evaluate & Rank Order
Ability to Learn
Attention to Detail
Draw Conclusions
Predict into Future
Understand
Understand Consequences
Communicate in a Foreign Language

Physical Resources: Circled _____ out of 29.
Sight
Hearing
Taste
Feeling
Smell
Walk
Run
Jog
Jump
Kinesthctics
Strength
Endurance
Lift & Carry
Flexibility
Kneel
Reach
Sit
Bend
Crouch
Push & Pull

Escaping Minimum Wage

    Grasp
    Manipulate
    Stand
    Drive an Automobile
    Ride a Bicycle, Motorcycle
    Drive Large Truck
    Pilot Airplane or Boat
    Deliver Items
    Aesthetics & Beauty

Spiritual Resources: Circled _____ out of 14.
    Belief in God
    Have Purpose
    Care for Earth
    God Will Guide
    Faith in Something Larger
    Ability to Center Self
    Reflection
    Reach Understanding
    Forgiveness
    Love of Plants
    Love of Animals
    Love of All Men
    Ability to Draw Strength
    Ability to Calm Self

Political Resources: Circled _____ out of 11.
    Right to Vote
    Ability to Influence
    Use of Power
    Make Decisions
    Understand Issues
    See Consequences
    Appreciate Minority View
    Leadership
    Being Prepared

Administrate
Encourage

Personal Relationship Resources: Circled _____ out of 21.
- Mentors
- Sponsors
- Teacher
- Counselor
- Clergy Member
- Spouse
- Boy/Girl Friend
- Best Friend
- Doctor
- Professor
- Parents
- Siblings
- Children
- Extended Family
- Friends
- Coworker
- Supervisor
- Neighbor
- Pet
- Service Animal
- Famous People

Support System: Circled _____ out of 17.
- Counselor
- Coworker
- Supervisor
- Health Clinic
- Doctor
- Neighbor
- Service Animal
- Police & Parole Officer
- Family

Friends
Public Transportation
Home Healthcare
Automobile
School
Cell Phone & Internet
Mail
Union

Class Standing

If you understand and feel comfortable doing each action below, circle its corresponding number. Transfer your circled numbers to the chart at the bottom. This quiz outlines how well you fit into a given socio-economic class by highlighting certain activities popular in each class. The more circles you have under one of the given classes helps you to quickly identify which class you instinctively gravitate towards.

1. I know how to get my children involved in baseball, piano lessons, soccer or cheerleading.
2. I know which rummage sales have "bag sales" and when.
3. I am on the boards of at least two charities.
4. I have several favorite restaurants in different countries of the world.
5. I know which grocery stores' trash bins can be accessed for discarded food.
6. I talk to my children about going to college.
7. I know which stores are most likely to carry the clothing brands my family wears.
8. I know how to keep my clothes from being stolen at the laundromat.
9. I understand the differences among principle, interest, and escrow on my mortgage.
10. I have at least two residences that are staffed and maintained.
11. I fly in my own plane or the company jet.
12. I support and buy the work of a particular artist.
13. I know how to help my children with their homework, and ask

the school for help as needed.
14. I know how to move in half a day.
15. I can get by without a car.
16. I know how to use checking, savings and a credit card.
17. I know how to physically fight and defend myself physically.
18. I know how to get a library card.
19. I know how to get a gun, even if I have a police record.
20. I know who my preferred financial advisor, attorney, interior designer, and accountant are.
21. I know how to read a corporate financial statement and analyze my own financial statements.
22. I know how to get someone out of jail.
23. I know how to use most of the tools in the garage.
24. I have at least two or three screens that keep people whom I do not wish to see away from me.

Poverty	Middle Class	Wealthy
2	1	3
5	6	4
8	7	10
14	9	11
15	13	12
17	16	20
19	18	21
22	23	24

This questionnaire is adapted from:
    Payne, Ruby, K. (2003). A framework for understanding poverty. 4th Ed. Aha! Process: Highlands, TX.

"Study not what the world is doing,
but what you can do for it."
Anon.

Chapter 6

Effect of Education

Blank (2011) says in *Changing Inequality*, "The United States is in an extended period of rapidly rising inequality. Starting in the mid-1970s, all measures of U.S. economic inequality have risen, including inequality in wages, income, and wealth." Understanding this fact is one thing, but it is quite another to change it. Level of education is one weapon a candidate can use to overcome inequality. Despite this, it appears that achievement of higher education by a candidate is related strongly, but not entirely, to how much education his/her parents achieved. Children tend to achieve the education and socio-economic levels their parents did. Nevertheless, the level of education one achieves is controllable by the candidate. If he/she has the motivation, college education is within reach of every high school graduate regardless of class ranking. Not all high school graduates who are highly motivated will earn a bachelor degree, but all of them are capable of a post-secondary certificate or Associate degree. What we know is that talent is different for each candidate. However, important job skills can be learned, and that is the key point. Just because a candidate's parents dropped out of high school does not mean he/she is not college material.

Below is Table 6-1 showing educational achievement (i.e., skill level) from 1979 (the turning point in equality) to 2007.

Table: 6-1: Educational Achievement Over Time		
Skill Level	1979	2007
Less than HS	24.6%	12.6%
High School	41.1%	29.8%
Some College	18.1%	29.5%
Bachelor Degree	11.9%	19.0%
Master or Higher	4.4%	9.2%

From this table, we see that over the past 28 years:
1. High School drop-outs have been cut by half,
2. Those stopping at high school have been significantly reduced,
3. Those getting Some College or an Associate degree have increased 63%,
4. About 1 in 5 now possess a Bachelor degree compared to about 1 in 10 in 1979,
5. Graduate and Professional degrees have more than doubled,
6. Overall, almost 58% have college experience in 2007 as compared to only about 34% in 1979.

Obviously, as a society, Americans today are achieving much greater educational credentials as compared to 1979. We are doing well in preventing high school drop-outs and encouraging high school graduates to continue their education in some sort of higher education. It would be interesting to see how many high school graduates stop their education at Some College / Associate degree on purpose. That is, as planned and not because of finances, lack of ability, or other factors.

Continuing with Blank (2011), she says, "This significant upward shift in the skills of the population raises median [annual] income by about $3,000." But what is striking is that while education levels on the whole have increased, which is good, it is this very fact that is contributing to inequality. How can that be? After all, we have been strongly encouraged to further our education, which, of course, we have done, and now we find that it leads to greater inequalities in society.

To understand this phenomenon, it is necessary to look at the interplay of several factors. First, the achievement of college degrees at or above the Bachelor level has increased from 16.3% in 1979 to 28.2% in 2007, which represents about a 73% increase. This is good, but it still only accounts for about one in three job candidates. A bachelor degree or higher remains the exception and not the rule. That is, they are more rare. Second, almost 100% of wage, income, and wealth increases have went solely to incumbents with a bachelor degree or higher. Businesses who employ college graduates have almost unanimously decided to financially reward the skills bachelor degree candidates bring to the job. Those candidates with less education have seen their incomes remain flat or decline slightly. In other words, income growth has not been equal across all skill levels. Third, the structure of the economy has limited those who do not possess advanced skills developed in college. Gone are well-paying jobs needing only a high school diploma. Manufacturing has declined, and in its place we now have low skilled, service jobs like restaurant work, housekeeping, and retailing that require only basic levels of education and ability. Inserting tab A into slot B is no longer well compensated. That went by the wayside once the manufacturing economy was replaced with the information economy. Right or wrong, business is not willing to pay these incumbents average wages, despite strong growth of productivity since 1979. Business pays its incumbents what it has to, not necessarily what they are worth. And in this transaction, those with less education are paid only at a level determined by their availability, which as we have seen is large representing about 2/3 of the labor-force. In effect, business makes more money on the skills of the college educated than it does off of the lower educated, and this fact is reflected in pay. As an exception, consider salespeople. They may or may not have formal training in college, but if they can sell and close the deal, they are paid very well. People are paid only what is necessary, meaning incumbents like social workers, elementary school teachers, and exercise physiologists make less than good salespeople who perhaps possess no education beyond high school. So when we say someone has a bachelor degree or higher, we mean they possess some type of skill that is both valuable in serving customers and makes money. It takes both to make good money. Consider the fortunes of professional athletes and Hollywood actors versus the plight of bakers and mechanics; we can do without baseball and movies, but society would grind to a halt without food and working machines, and yet these groups are paid enormously different salaries. To conclude, understand that college education (i.e., skill level) helps produce inequality because its graduates are still few, those who possess degrees are paid more for their skills because they bring in much more revenue, the market only pays what it has to, and the success of the economy has aligned with the success of people who are educated and possess valuable skills.

"Nothing is work unless you'd
rather be doing something else."
George Halas

Table: 6-2: Actual Skill Level of Population (1)

Education Level	Millions of Candidates	Percent of Population
Less than HS	29.6	13%
High School	70.0	30%
Some College	46.5	20%
Associate Degree	22.2	9%
Bachelor Degree	44.4	19%
Master Degree	17.6	7%
Doctor Degree	6.5	3%

(1) census.gov/hhes/socdemo/education/data/cps/2013/tables.html

Table: 6-3: Education Required for Entry (2)

Education Level	Millions of Jobs	Percent of 132.4m Jobs
Less than HS	36.1	27%
High School	51.5	39%
Some College	9.7	7%
Associate Degree	5.7	4%
Bachelor Degree	23.8	18%
Master Degree	2.2	2%
Doctor Degree	3.4	3%

(2) bls.gov/spotlight/2014/occupations/home.htm

Table: 6-4: Incumbents Participating by Skill Level

Education	Participation Rate	Total Candidates	Total Incumbents
Less than HS	45%	29.6 m	13.3 m
High School	59%	70.0 m	41.3 m
Some or AS	67%	68.7 m	46.0 m
Bachelor +	75%	68.5 m	51.4 m

Table: 6-5: Ratio of Jobs to Participants by Skill Level

Education	Millions of Jobs	Number of Participants	Ratio of Jobs to Participants
Less than HS	36.1 m	13.3 m	2.71 X
High School	51.5 m	41.3 m	1.25 X
Some or AS	15.4 m	46.0 m	0.33 X
Bachelor +	29.4 m	51.4 m	0.57 X

Escaping Minimum Wage

The actual numbers in the tables above are not as important as noting the general trends. Five such trends are examined below. First, as education level increases there is a concomitant rise in participation rates by candidates. Less than one in two candidates hold jobs when their skill development ends before attaining a high school diploma. This is true despite there being almost three jobs available for each candidate that has less than a high school diploma. Opportunity is not what is keeping these candidates out of the labor market, as there are plenty of open jobs. Clearly, it is something else, like perhaps, their motivation to work, their values concerning work, their ability to do the work available to them, or the lack of enough incentive to persist in work. On the other hand, three of four bachelor degree holders or higher possess jobs. Opportunity might explain why only 75% have jobs, as there is a lack of enough jobs to go around. Numerically, there are about 51 million qualified candidates, but only about 30 million jobs available that require an advanced degree. This fact is often overlooked and it is probably the reason why America has 15,000 bachelor degree holders who are parking lot attendants and 40,000 bachelor degree holders who are building cleaners. As skill level goes up, participation in work goes up.

Second, more jobs exist at lower skill levels that require only a high school diploma or less. Numerically, there are about 88 million jobs available for 100 million possible candidates, but because of a blended, low participation rate of about 55% there are only about 55 million motivated incumbents. This leaves 33 million jobs to be filled by incumbents with more education, meaning they will be under-employed. This results in lower wages for incumbents who have struggled through college, whether for a certificate, associate degree or bachelor degree or higher.

Third, there are not enough jobs available for candidates who have trained in college. The blended ratio is about two candidates for each job. Clearly, if those left over want to work, they must take jobs below their skill level. Under-employment is a fact of life for many college graduates.

Fourth, highly educated candidates displace lower educated ones. This occurs because given two candidates for a job, the business tends to favor the one with a college education. This is not wrong. It simply means the business is making a strategic decision to employ the candidate best able to fulfill the tasks required of the job. It comes down to economics where a rational decision is made about who can best bring in more income than what he/she costs. Interestingly, this phenomenon points to the fact that the business gets to use the college-gained skills of the incumbent even when he/she is employed in a position not requiring a college degree. For example, consider an incumbent with a biology degree who works at a pet store selling fish, mice, and birds. The rate of pay for a position is determined by the scope of tasks to be done, and not by the level of education that the particular incumbent possesses.

Fifth, higher educated candidates can take jobs at or below the required skill level. That is, they usually start at the top and work their way down until employed. Lower educated candidates usually cannot take jobs above their skill level. This may be reflected in participation rates. In short, higher educated candidates have more work options available to them, so they tend to have higher participation rates.

One of the easiest ways to get ahead in America is by furthering your education. Americans love to get jobs by earning degrees. In fact educational attainment has a large, positive correlation with socio-economic class. It is also probably safe to assume that education level causes incumbents to gravitate toward one particular socio-economic class. This is good news because a diligent student with help from key adults, like parents or teachers, can progress up the educational continuum as far as he/she wants. In other words, the student may not be able to influence the class she/he was born in to, but can certainly influence how high he/she goes in school. So it seems education is a major dividing line regardless if that is good or bad.

If you do not have a high school degree, the most effective way to boost your standing is to get your diploma or General Education Development (GED). It is easier to do now than it was in the past because teaching methods have been refined and it much more convenient, as many cities have both day and night programs. It is widely recognized, improves prestige, and demonstrates your motivation. It also gives you the first major educational credential showing competence and a basic level of knowledge and skill. However, even without a high school diploma or GED there are many things you can do to get ahead.

Less than High School Diploma
(representative, not exhaustive)

1. Craft & Fine Artists
2. Fashion Designers
3. Floral Designers
4. Grounds Maintenance Workers
5. Janitors & Building Cleaners
6. Maids & Housekeepers
7. Construction Laborers
8. Oil & Gas Workers
9. Painters
10. Plasterers
11. Roofers
12. Tile Setters
13. Self-enrichment Teacher
14. Actors
15. Professional Athlete
16. Dancers
17. Musicians & Singers
18. Agricultural Workers
19. Fishers
20. Bartenders
21. Cooks
22. Food Servers
23. Food Preparation Workers
24. Dishwashers
25. Interpreters
26. Couriers & Messengers
27. Bakers
28. Meat Cutters
29. Laundry Workers
30. Sewers & Tailors
31. Meat Packers
32. Security Guards
33. Cashiers

34. Modeling
35. Retail Sales Workers
36. Salesperson
37. Hand Laborers
38. Material Movers
39. Trash Collectors
40. Taxi Drivers
41. Small Business Owner

Table: 6-6: Jobs Requiring Less than HS Diploma

Advantages	Disadvantages
No Diploma Required	Low Pay
Flexible Schedule	Low Responsibility
No After-work Demands	Little Autonomy
Only Low Skills Needed	Limited Skill Development
Highly Prescribed Work	Very High Turn-over Rate
Lots of Guidance/Supervision	Low Prestige
Honest work for Honest Pay	Can Be Boring for Some
Stepping-stone to Better Jobs	Can Be Physically Demanding
Potential for Advancement	Higher Risk for Injury
Temporary Jobs	
Learn Basic Work Responsibilities	
Many Openings	
Easy to Get Hired	
Always in Demand	
Good Fall-Back Position	
Training On-the-Job	
No Experience Necessary	
Below Average Intelligence is Okay	

There is absolutely nothing wrong with any of the above positions. They offer work needing to be done. If you do not want to pursue an education, tend to take the view that there more to life than work, and can live on lower wages, then these are good options. You can bounce around from employer to employer, as you desire with no real ramifications for doing so. Nevertheless, when you find something you like, say, a certain job or work schedule, it is best to stay put. There are many candidates who would also like that position for the very same reasons you do.

Many incumbents who have worked jobs like these eventually want more. Whether it is pay, responsibility, or autonomy, many choose to use these jobs to gain entry-level work skills and then move on, often upward. In fact there is solid evidence, albeit anecdotal, that candidates who have worked in "fast food" take on decidedly better positions later in life precisely because of the training and skills gained at the typical restaurant. "Fast food" is not easy work. There is customer service, cashiering and counting money, and following directions, all of which demand more of the incumbent than, say, something like housekeeping. Just because society expects you to have at least a high school education, does not mean there are not viable alternatives. Your job is to contribute anyway you can. A life lived as a happy, productive trash collector is far better than a life lived as a miserable, incompetent middle manager.

If, however, you do not mind schooling and working full-time, a much better existence might be had with a High School Diploma, GED, Certificate, Associate or Bachelor degree. Each of these opens new doors not available to those who did not finish high school. The jobs, advantages, and disadvantages for each of these are given below.

Jobs Qualified-for with a High School Diploma
(not exhaustive, but representational)

1. Surveyors & Mapping Technicians
2. Pest Control Workers
3. Real Estate Appraisers
4. Insurance Claims Adjusters
5. Loan Officer

6. Social Service Assistants
7. Substance Abuse Counselors
8. Boilermakers
9. Blockmasons
10. Carpenters
11. Carpet Installers
12. Cement Masons
13. Building Inspectors
14. Construction Equipment Operators
15. Drywall Installers
16. Electrician
17. Hazardous Materials Removers
18. Iron Workers
19. Library Assistants
20. Teacher Assistants
21. Coaches & Scouts
22. Umpires & Referees
23. Forest Workers
24. Logging Workers
25. Chefs
26. Home Health Aide
27. Medical Assistants
28. Occupational Health Technicians
29. Opticians
30. Pharmacy Technicians
31. Psychiatric Technicians
32. Veterinary Assistants
33. Farmer & Ranch Management
34. Food Service Managers
35. Legislators
36. Hospitality Managers
37. Real Estate Managers
38. Photographers
39. U.S.A. Military Enlisted
40. Office Support Workers
41. U.S.A. Postal Workers

42. Most Production Workers
43. Correctional Officers
44. Most Sales Positions
45. Water Transportation Workers

Table: 6-7: Jobs Requiring Only a High School Diploma	
Advantages	**Disadvantages**
On-the-Job Training	Physically Demanding
Average Pay	Average Pay
Full-time Work	Average Prestige
Flexible Schedules	Possible Poor Working Conditions
More Autonomy	Limited Advancement
Less Supervision	Some Risk for Injury
Middle Skills Needed	
Average Intelligence Used	
Little Experience Needed	
Good Fall-back Position	
Easy to Get Hired	
Many Openings	
Good Stepping-stone to Better Work	
Usually in Demand	
Requires Some Skill Development	
Lower Turn-over Rates	
Average Prestige	

If you desire more specific training that high school does not offer, earning a Post-Secondary Certificate is a good, first step. These tend to be very specialized, which can be a benefit and a potential disadvantage. A certificate opens doors to very specific jobs; however, over time the labor market may change, making your certificate obsolete, but on the other hand, community colleges that offer certificates tend to know what is employable in the local area. Despite this, it is the responsibility of the candidate to have a plan about why she wants the certificate. In other words, if you get a certificate in X, then you expect to work only in X. Listed below are some certificates, after that, some advantages and disadvantages.

Certificates
(not exhaustive, but representational)

1. State-tested Nursing Aides
2. State-tested Pest Control Workers
3. Real Estate Salesperson
4. Loan Officers
5. Personal Income Tax Preparers
6. Computer Support Specialists
7. Hazardous Materials Workers
8. Dental Assistants
9. Paramedics & EMTs
10. Licensed Practical Nurses
11. Licensed Vocational Nurses
12. Massage Therapists
13. Medical Records Technicians
14. Medical Transcriptionists
15. Psychiatric Technicians
16. Surgical Technologists
17. Court Reporters
18. Accounting Clerks
19. Administrative Assistants
20. Firefighters
21. Private Detectives

22. Salespersons
23. Flight Attendants

Table: 6-8: Jobs Requiring a Post-secondary Certificate	
Advantages	**Disadvantages**
Fastest Way to More Income	Potential for Obsolescence
Specialization in One Occupation	Requires Education
Middle Skills Necessary	Training Costs Money
More Responsibility	Possible After-work Demands
Less Supervision	
Seen as Expert	
Good Stepping-stone to Higher Degrees	
Good Number of Openings	
Usually in Demand	
Good Fall-back Position	
More Communication Skills Needed	
Opportunity for Advancement	
Advanced Skill Development	
Lower Turn-over Rates	
Rising Prestige	
Less Physically Demanding	
Less Risk for Injury	
Usually Long-term Employment	
Usually Daytime Schedule	

An Associate Degree is the first degree level offered in American Higher Education. It requires four semesters of full-time study, and almost always demands an experiential component, such as an internship, co-op, on-the-job training, shadow experience or informational interview. One of the advantages of earning an Associate degree is that it is usually transferable to a four-year institution where the student enters as a junior. This can be a very cost effective way of obtaining both degrees because community colleges typically charge much less for a credit-hour than a four-year college or university. Also, by first completing the Associate degree and then the Baccalaureate degree, means the student has two high-quality professions from which to choose. This is very advantageous when recessions in the economy hit one or the other occupation particularly hard. In other words, you have successfully diversified your skills so that you are always employable no matter the health of the greater labor market. Listed below is common Associate degree professions along with advantages and disadvantages.

Associate Degree Professionals
(not exhaustive, but representational)

1. Aerospace Engineering Technicians
2. Civil Engineering Technicians
3. Drafters
4. Electrical Engineering Technicians
5. Electro-Mechanical Technicians
6. Environmental Engineering Technicians
7. Industrial Engineering Technicians
8. Mechanical Engineering Technicians
9. Library Technicians
10. Preschool Teachers
11. Cardiovascular Technologists
12. Dental Hygienists
13. Diagnostic medical Sonographers
14. Clinical Laboratory Technicians
15. Nuclear Medicine Technologists
16. Occupational Therapist Assistants

17. Physical Therapist Assistants
18. Radiation Therapists
19. Radiologic Technologists
20. Registered Nurses
21. Respiratory Therapists
22. Veterinary Technologists
23. Paralegals
24. Food Science Technicians
25. Chemical Technicians
26. Environmental Science Technicians
27. Forest & Conservation Technicians
28. Geological & Petroleum Technicians
29. Nuclear Technicians
30. Construction Managers
31. Broadcast & Sound Technicians
32. Desktop Publishers
33. Administrative Assistants
34. Air-Traffic Controllers
35. Surgical Technologist
36. Pharmacy Technologist
37. Massage Therapist
38. Fitness Instructor
39. Welder
40. Machinist

Avoid these postsecondary certificates:
1. Accounting: Requires a Bachelor Degree
2. Bookkeepers: Only Need a HS Diploma
3. Kindergarten Teacher: Requires a Bachelor Degree
4. Human Resources: Need Associate or Bachelor Degree
5. Marketing: Requires Bachelor Degree
6. Paralegal: Requires Associate or Bachelor Degree

Table: 6-9: Jobs Requiring an Associate Degree	
Advantages	**Disadvantages**
Degree Required	Degree Required
Less Supervision	After-work Demands
More Autonomy	Cost of Training
Stepping-stone to BA	Time Required for Training
Requires Above Average Intelligence	Possibility of Obsolescence
Requires Above Average Commitment	
Excellent Fall-back Position	
Usually in Demand	
Excellent Pay for Commitment	
Skill Growth Opportunity	
Room to Advance	
More Responsibility	
Lower Turn-over Rates	
Good Prestige	
Less Physically Demanding	

"Every man dies. Not every man really lives."
William Wallace

Escaping Minimum Wage

A bachelor degree is often seen as the minimum degree requirement to be a professional. It requires eight semesters of full-time study plus two or more practical experiences, such as an internship or co-op. It is essential to obtain practical work experience before graduation to be considered for the best positions. It is also the gateway to Graduate study, such as Master's, Doctoral, or First Professional Degrees. Many candidates end formal education with this degree, but still maintain continuing education to stay abreast of developments in the profession.

A BA is considered the passport to the middle class. It encompasses most middle-wage, middle-skill jobs. Unemployment is very low, and most positions weather recessions well. Salary is high, especially with five or more years of experience in one area. Employers have been, and continue to prefer to hire Bachelor degree candidates because they possess the complex skills required on the job. Some of these skills include writing, speaking, computing, listening, problem solving, and professional attitude. As American society gains more education with more specialization, it is more common for BA holders to displace incumbents with lesser degrees and experience. This shows the reason why BA holders have low unemployment rates even in recessions. However, it is also more common for BA holders to work in jobs that do not require a bachelor degree. This happens for two main reasons. First, America's colleges and universities often produce too many graduates in certain areas. Consider Elementary Education (an excess) versus Petroleum Engineers (a deficit). Second, too many bachelor degree holders have poor experience records because the schools do not require it. Yet, this is changing yearly. If you want the most efficiency and effectiveness of a given BA degree, it is best to have experience, good contacts in the field, and a certification or license *in addition to the degree.* Certification and licensure exclude, by definition, all other candidates who do not possess one. This keeps many people out of the profession, helping to keep salaries high, unemployment low, and opportunities plentiful. Nevertheless, a liberal arts BA degree is also just as valuable as one that is licensed, but for a different reason than exclusion. A liberal arts degree is more general and builds better foundational skills for many different professions. It is also much less likely to become out-dated. In the final analysis, carefully consider the BA degree you get. Be sure the graduates before you have achieved what you would like to achieve. Of course, you may have different goals, but a Certified Financial Analyst (a specific, vocational degree) is unlikely to become a Historian (a liberal arts degree) and vice versa. Below are professions requiring a BA. After that is a summary of advantages and disadvantages.

Jobs Requiring a Bachelor Degree
(representative not exhaustive)

1. Aerospace Engineers
2. Agricultural Engineers
3. Architects
4. Biomedical Engineers
5. Chemical Engineers
6. Civil Engineers
7. Computer Hardware Engineers
8. Electrical Engineers
9. Industrial Engineers
10. Mechanical Engineers
11. Art Directors
12. Graphic Designers
13. Industrial Designers
14. Accountants
15. Budget Analysts
16. Human Resources Specialists
17. Insurance Underwriters
18. Markey Research Analysts
19. Personal Financial Advisors
20. Purchasing Managers
21. Health Educators
22. Social Workers
23. Computer Programmers
24. Computer Systems Analysts
25. Adult Literacy Teachers
26. High School Teachers
27. Special Education Teachers

28. Athletic Trainers
29. Dieticians & Nutritionists
30. Recreational therapists
31. Food Scientists
32. Atmospheric scientists
33. Chemists
34. Economists
35. Forensic Science Technicians
36. Geoscientists
37. Microbiologists
38. Survey researchers
39. Zoologists
40. Marketing Managers
41. Financial Managers
42. Medical Services Managers
43. Public Relations Managers
44. Actuaries
45. Editors & Authors
46. U.S.A. Military Officers
47. Sales Engineers
48. Financial Services Sales Agents
49. K-8 Teachers
50. News Analysts

"Try not to become a man of success,
but rather try to become a man of value."
Albert Einstein

Table: 6-10: Jobs Requiring a Bachelor Degree or Higher	
Advantages	**Disadvantages**
High Pay	Potential for Long Work Weeks
Low Unemployment	Excessive Travel
High Prestige	Requires Degree
Good Openings	Requires Time to Train
Middle Skills Needed	Risk of Underemployment
Lots of Autonomy	Requires Continuing Education
Limited Supervision	Possibility of Obsolescence
Stepping-stone to Graduate Degree	Sometimes Difficult to Get Hired
Usually in Demand	
Requires Above Average Intelligence	
Requires Desire to Work	
Job Outlook Excellent	
Good Work Environment	
Seen as Expert in Field	
Much Room for Promotion	
Satisfying Career-path	
Low Risk of Injury	

First, finish high school or earn your GED. Almost all jobs require this, and the ones that do not are low paying, highly dictated positions. For example, many of these jobs are in general labor, food service, and cleaning. There is nothing wrong with any of these; they are honest work for an honest wage, albeit only minimum wage. These positions offer a lot of opportunity for a lot of candidates just starting out. Turnover, a measure of length of tenure, is very high in these positions as compared to higher skill jobs. People who start their careers in these occupations learn to use them as stepping-stones to better positions. However, if you have no high school diploma, desire an easy job to get and keep, enjoy work that is highly prescribed, want flexible schedules with little after-work demands, then these jobs suit your needs.

As an adolescent or young adult, you should thoroughly explore your interests and career aspirations well before making a choice. This is especially true if you might lower your career expectations. Because once done so, this compromise tends to overly limit the range of careers available to you later on. When you are young, get as much education as possible. It will never work against you. Try not to let your current circumstances, current abilities, any perceived barriers to entry, or thoughts of future opportunities force you to make a career choice that requires limited education and lands you in poverty. You do not have to possess all the abilities a certain career demands up-front. School will teach you. Ask yourself: About aspirations: "What occupation would I do if there were no limiting factors?" About expectations: "What occupation am I likely to enter given all that I know at this point?" See if you can make your answers agree with each other.

School places an over-emphasis on IQ, yet we find that intelligence quotient offers little to explain different destinies of people with roughly equal promise. Often those with a high IQ are not more successful, not paid more, not happier, nor more satisfied with life than those who are merely average. Despite this, we continue to measure IQ as if it really told us something worth while. And the fact of the matter is that it probably ends up limiting true talent and desire to achieve in those who might see a different path.

Escaping Minimum Wage

A much better alternative given that a lot of knowledge is becoming obsolete at an accelerated rate is to teach our high school graduates how to think for themselves. That is, they should be able to utilize and assimilate new information, reason, draw conclusions, communicate those conclusions, and make decisions in the face of incomplete information.

James (2012) in *The College Wage Premium* from the Federal Reserve Bank of Cleveland examined the effect of college major and attainment of a graduate degree on the College Wage Premium over similar students who stopped their education with high school graduation. He says, "Current data indicate that college degree holders enjoy an 84% increase in earnings over their high school educated counterparts."

James goes on to discover that certain majors are paid much more than others, and we should not lump all bachelor degree holders together when examining college wage premium. He finds the highest wage premium for: Engineering, Computers & Mathematics, Healthcare, Business, and Physical Science. Using his data, we find the college wage premium over high school graduates to be 20% for 'Some College, No Degree', 65% for 'Bachelor Degrees', and 115% for those with advanced, graduate degrees.

"Our life always expresses the
result of our dominant thoughts."
Soren Kierkegaard

Escaping Minimum Wage

Warren Buffett, the 2nd richest man in America, talks of investing in companies that have a "Wide-Moat." He means these companies have a competitive advantage that protects their market and sales. For example, American Electric Power or Microsoft both are businesses that are well-protected from competition because it is very difficult or impossible to enter their market.

Using this idea in choosing a profession we get:

1. Choose a profession that is something most people cannot do for themselves, like getting a hair-cut, doing electrical repairs, or investing for retirement.

2. Choose a profession that has a foundation that is not a fad, but rather, is always needed, such as mortuary science, statistician, or library science.

3. Choose a profession requiring a college degree, the higher, the better. Consider a bachelor degree for mechanical engineering, a master degree for counseling, or a doctorate for college teaching and research.

4. Choose a profession that requires licensure, certification, or membership in a union. Consider board-certified for a physician, certification for a financial analyst, or union membership for automobile assembly.

5. Choose a profession where you can use a rare talent. Consider singing, playing a sport, playing an instrument, doing surgery, selling insurance, doing scientific research, or inventing a new product or process.

6. Choose a profession that makes use of exclusive network and contact resources. Once you get beyond entry-level positions, your reputation and network contacts go far in determining how high up the hierarchy you progress. People do not get powerful positions on their own; it takes a helping hand.

7. Choose a profession that cannot be out-sourced, off-shored, or automated, like construction, hospitality, or food service.

Professions with wide moats tend to have stable earnings and steady demand where the incumbent is protected in difficult financial times. The more of these 'wide-moat' features you utilize the better off you are likely to be.

Summary

The reason why a high school diploma is not as valuable as it once was is because it is a generalist degree in a job market that demands refined knowledge, skill, and ability. If you stop your education with high school, it is imperative that you have a plan to capitalize on a passionate talent. Then, with time you can become more specialized, which happens to be the main component of a college degree. Whether you go to work after high school or enroll in college, dues in the form of specialized knowledge formed around a set of skills must be earned.

When you graduate from this period of time, you probably possess enough diversified information so you can offer benefits to an employer. Do not mistake a feature as a benefit. Although related, a feature is your BA degree, but a benefit is the reason an employer will hire you, say, an ability to close sales. In effect, your talent is the answer to the employer's problems. Far too many candidates feel entitled to a job when they only feature a degree and not really a valuable benefit the customer will pay for.

Remember in any job (except government) you must bring in more profit than what you cost, otherwise there is no incentive to keep paying you. That is, you lose your job. To be successful you must offer something better, faster, unique or more convenient than what the other 19 applicants for a particular job do. If all you do is insert Tab A into Slot B, do not expect to be richly rewarded. True value comes from the marriage of talent within an execution of skill that is in demand.

"Success is a lousy teacher. It seduces
smart people into thinking they can't lose."
Bill Gates

Chapter 7

Ownership

Ownership of key assets is almost crucial for long-term success. Owning a credential, an education, a business, a home, a car, savings, ideas, and your life in general bring advantages not acquired when renting, leasing, borrowing, or using something that is not yours. Renting is most often a temporary solution to a permanent problem. It almost always costs more and gives you fewer options in the long run. Usually by owning something there is lower risk and a greater chance of getting ahead. Presented below are several things you can own to enhance your life through wealth, security, health, and happiness.

Skill based on Talent

One of the best things to own is a skill based on your best talent. Taking a talent and honing it with the use of a skill over time is one of life's greatest pleasures, which also happens to be the best way to make a living. We all have a strong tendency to enjoy what we are good at, and we are good at what we enjoy; however, there are exceptions. This is a very good thing because in your proficiency you do something for others that they are unable to do for themselves. Likewise others do things they are good at, for you, which you might not be good at. This relationship is the basis for our modern economy. We each have unique talents, and we trade among us so everyone gets what they need from the person who does it best.

How do you own a skill based around your talent? To begin, it is necessary to take inventory of what you enjoy and what you do well. You might, at first, enjoy something, but not be the best at it. That is okay. A strength is just something that fills you with energy and power, and as you go you get better and better. On the other hand, a weakness is just something that drains you of vitality, and which you do not enjoy. Given these two definitions, it is quite possible to be good at a weakness and bad at a strength. Consider the following examples. Could not someone be great at mathematics but find it a total bore? Could not someone be a poor golfer but really enjoy it? The answer is, obviously, yes. The point is talent is something innate to us, whereas skill is something learned. And fortunately for us, most things in life can be learned. But real power, meaning, and satisfaction come from something that combines talent and skill into one end product. Consider Einstein's ability to see pictures in his head combined with mathematics, Thoreau's ability to distill meaning from the woods and turn it into the book called *Walden*, or Buffet's ability to find undervalued companies and combine it with his and others' capital investment for outstanding growth of wealth. To summarize point one, find your talents, which you probably are already aware of, then ask yourself by what skill can I engage my talent, which might be more difficult to figure out. When you answer these questions, you have found a strength you can rely on for untold success.

Next, examine where and how you can develop skills to own. In this area, reference education (i.e., high school & college), the trades (e.g., carpentry, plumbing, or electrician), selling (e.g., selling cars, furniture, or insurance), and volunteering (e.g., at hospital, kindergarten, or library). Each of these has its advantages, in the form of opportunities, and disadvantages, in the form of what you must give up, as well as required time, effort, and risk.

Own a College Degree

Earning a college degree is a popular way of combining a talent with a skill. Owning a college degree opens many doors previously held shut. It certifies that you have the necessary vocabulary, experience, social skill, ability to communicate, ability to use mathematics, think abstractly, and contribute to the success of businesses, organizations, or government. When you make the decision to go to college, you are making the commitment to work for a living. College has been called the passport to the middle class, and the middle class works in the professions.

Owning a college degree, especially one that confers a recognized credential or license, is a powerful way to make your skills valuable. By definition, a degree with a license or certification means you are proficient at performing a specific job that others without the credential are excluded from doing. This does five things for you. First, it limits the number of candidates who are legally allowed to practice that profession. Second, it helps to keep incumbents' salary and benefits high. Third, it helps ensure incumbents with the credential are professional, competent, responsible, and up-to-date on the necessary knowledge, skill, and abilities. Fourth, the credential means you are an expert in your area. It conveys trust and helps ensure standards in the profession. Finally, owning a college degree is permanent and cannot be taken from you like an object.

Going to college is not something to be taken lightly. There are many valid reasons why students go to college. Perhaps, they want to learn more about subjects that interest them, they want to grow personally and professionally, they want to party and find a mate, or they simply follow their friends because they have not thought of doing anything different. Some of these are better than others but in today's economy, however, a majority of students that enroll in college do so because it helps them find and establish a good career.

If you are going to college to get a good job after graduation, the following discussion outlines some of the more important things to consider before making definite plans.

Escaping Minimum Wage

To begin, look at your values concerning work:
1. Do you believe work is not just a way to make money?
2. Do you highly value professional work and are willing to invest 45-60 hours per week on your career?
3. Do you desire work that is complex and full of responsibility?
4. Have you ruled-out careers in the trades or lower skilled service jobs?
5. Are you highly motivated to engage in lifetime learning in your career area?

Secondly, evaluate opportunity cost. That is, if you go to college and become a professional then there are certain things you give up in exchange.
1. Are you willing to invest four to six years of your time to earn a degree?
2. Are you willing to work in your degree area for many years? After all, if you become a dentist, what else are you expected to do for a living?
3. Are you willing to spend many thousands of dollars, sometimes repaying debt over 10 or 25 years, to acquire the necessary knowledge, skill, experience, and formal licensure to be a professional?
4. Are you certain you really want to be a professional instead of working as little as possible and enjoying the simple pleasures in life?

Finally, do you think you will be successful in college and as a professional with a dedicated career?
1. Are you, or can you learn to be, a good communicator in the standard areas consisting of reading, writing, speaking, mathematics, science, and technology?
2. Are you able to learn complex skills and detailed knowledge, and then execute them in a highly structured work environment?
3. Did you graduate in the top half of your high school class? If no, are you highly motivated to succeed in remedial coursework in college?
4. Can you specifically identify a talent you wish to exploit as a professional?

If you cannot answer most of these questions with a "yes," you are best advised to reconsider why you want to go to college. It may be that you simply have always been told you should go to college if you want a good job. But you should understand there is probably no single best career you must do for a living. There are other options if you will just look. Make your decision with thought and reflection on what you are really talented at and really want to do to make a living.

Own a Trade Skill

If you are not enthusiastic about college, another popular way of owning a skill based around your talent is to enter the trades. Many men, and a few women, who are good with their hands find this route to be very satisfying. It takes about the same number of years to become a journeyman as it does to earn a BA and Master degree. The trades are in construction and maintenance, such as block-mason, sheet metal worker, painter, and carpenter, to name a few. Since 1976 colleges and universities have enrolled and graduated more women than men (55% vs. 45%) precisely because men have options like the trades. The trades, which employ apprentices and journeymen, are somewhat insulated from labor market fluctuations because most belong to a union. And when the economy sours and construction is postponed, the workers rely on the union for work in their city or a nearby city. The trades are protected because they require long training and membership to a union, which keeps salary high and avoids competition from workers without the journeyman credential.

Own the Ability to Sell

Another good option to match a talent with a skill is in sales. Sales is a viable option if you are good at talking, listening, and negotiating. Although you can go to college to learn the profession, what it really comes down to is whether or not you can convince a customer to buy for reasons he values. Excellent salespeople are very well compensated and there really is not much of a ceiling to what can be earned. In fact according to Brian Tracy, salespeople and entrepreneurs account for 80% of all millionaires in America.

Own the Ability to Communicate
If you stopped your education when you graduated from high school, do not despair. High school gives you a solid grounding in how to communicate. Consider classes like English, foreign languages, computers, mathematics, science, and history. All of these contribute to your ability to relate and communicate no matter the job or career you pursue. Reflect on which classes you really enjoyed and were good at; and, these may lead you to discover your best talent and which you can then combine with a skill of your choosing.

If you have no diploma or degree, strongly consider getting at least a GED. Here again, it matters if you have a minimum of education. The high school diploma or GED is the de facto required degree for almost all jobs. Not having one often eliminates you for a job way before interviews are scheduled. Nevertheless, if you dropped out of high school, you still have opportunities to match a talent with a skill. One such opportunity is one that you create, volunteering. If you are courageous, persistent, and possess a positive attitude, many businesses or organizations will accept and create a volunteer just for you. Consider hospitals, social service agencies, the government, and for-profit businesses that interest you. Then, ask and ask again. Many will not turn you away but it is up to you to take the first few steps and demonstrate your motivation and worth.

Summary of Owning a Skill
Owning a skill around a talent and having proof you can use it, is your ability to earn a living. It is a common path where incumbents work 40 hours a week as employees. The options one has without owning a skill is bleak, usually ending in low-skilled, low pay service jobs that have limited futures. A college degree, trade, sales-position, volunteer opportunity, and even a high school diploma with focus go a long way in securing a job that brings in decent money, steady work, and other opportunities in due time. Owning a skill means you offer an employer developed ability, which is increasingly valued in today's complex and competitive economy. It is clear, hopefully, that everyone who works for a living, which includes almost everyone (i.e., 99%+), would do well to develop a marketable skill around his best talent.

Ownership of a Business

America is the land of opportunity, more specifically the opportunity to own a business. Nowhere else is everyone an entrepreneur from starting a fledgling business to garage sales, it seems everyone participates. Our laws, open-market structure, and attitude make the U.S. the land of opportunity and one of the few places where the disadvantaged can go from rags to riches in the same generation. In fact, almost all millionaires are self-made in one generation and owning a business is among the few reasons why. Furthermore, business entrepreneurship and business management rank first as majors for undergraduates in America's colleges and universities. More than 20% of all degrees conferred in a typical year are to students majoring in business. A well-run business with an idea that drives its competitive advantage allows the owner, whether a sole-proprietor or stock shareholder, to receive all the profits. Of course, the owner also assumes all of the risk of loss at the same time.

The ownership of business pays off most when the owner builds it around his interests and on top of his talent. Consider Wal-mart and the Walton family, Apple and Steve Jobs and Facebook with Marc Zuckerburg. They all had an idea, a vision, and assumed the risk of failure but reaped huge profits in short order.

An alternate way of owning a business that is also very successful is to buy a franchise of an existing, proven business. McDonald's, Papa John's Pizza, and Best Western Hotel are all franchise businesses that offer a standardized business model with proven success. The owner may or may not have a novel idea or much talent above average, but that does not matter. The idea for success has already been figured out. The heavy lifting has been done, yet it still takes dedication and some talent to succeed in each new application of the franchise. Nevertheless, ownership of the business enables success way beyond just being an employee.

A business built around a profession and the purchase of an existing business are other ways to own a key asset. The former includes people like physicians, accountants, and plumbers whereas the latter could be any business. However, a sharp distinction is drawn between the two. A business built around a profession is difficult to sell because only a professional in the same area could reap the rewards of the business. The business is the interest and talent of the professional. On the other hand, a hardware store or fitness club can easily be sold to someone else and still have the structure necessary to be successful in its own right.

Owning a Home

A third key asset to own for wealth, security and enjoyment is to own your home or condominium. We all have to live somewhere. And even though it is a large expense, it is also the most popular way of accruing an asset. A home that you own has long been part of the American dream. It gives you a steady place to live and a sense of accomplishment. As they say, they are not making any more land. And if you are lucky enough to own some in a desirable place (i.e., think location, location, location), you are likely to realize real gains, which can set up a whole host of other developments, including owning a business. A home, generally, increases in value. And with equity, you can borrow against it to fund other things you want. As pointed out in the opening, renting a place to live is a temporary solution to a permanent need. Despite this, sometimes renting a place is a good idea, such as if you are not ready to settle in one area. On the whole, however, owning your home is much more advantageous if only for the possibilities it gives you.

Owning a Car

Owning your own car is a step towards security and enjoyment, if not a little wealth. Here again, transportation is an on-going problem that is temporarily solved with leasing a car. Leasing a new car is one solution that probably drains your bank account. With a lease and successive leases, you always have to make a payment on something you do not own. You realize little or no equity and always have a persistent liability. Naturally, there are legitimate reasons to lease an automobile that make sense. But one of them is not to save money. Owning a car that you can use in any manner you wish along with the fact that it is yours to keep once paid for makes ownership a valued option that pays off in the long run.

Escaping Minimum Wage

Fungible Assets

The next asset to own, which many people do not possess, is savings that grows faster than inflation. Savings may take the form of a 401k, 403b, IRA, taxable brokerage account, real estate, or collectibles like coins, bullion, stamps, art, autographs, antiques and just about anything that is valuable and rare. Included here is the category of intellectual property, such as inventions and patents, music performed, and books written, among others. Each class of investment has its own advantages and potential risks, but over time these almost always outperform cash. Stocks, bonds, mutual funds, and real estate tend to consistently produce gains better than inflation, which make them good places to store money for future use. Except for real estate and collectibles, they are very liquid, meaning they can be turned into cash almost immediately. Of course, their values depend on the economy and to a larger extent the performance of individual companies that issue stock. But the stock market has never lost money in any 20-year, rolling period of time. Despite this, a large number of people do not trust the stock market because they think it is rigged against them in favor of the rich. Many procrastinate and therefore lose out on amassing wealth by compounding interest, dividends, and capital gains. This is especially true for the younger workers who came of age during the Great Recession. Make no mistake, you will end up with less if you do not invest your money in one of these vehicles, and instead rely on savings accounts and certificates of deposit. A good strategy is to begin slowly and learn about the different ways to invest. It does not matter as much what you invest in at the beginning. It is more important to open an account, like a Roth IRA, and fund it. There will be plenty of time to allocate your owned assets as you go. Remember you lose 100% plus any gains of the money you do not save.

"The starting point of all achievement is desire."
Napoleon Hill

Live the Life Only You Can Live
The final asset you must own is your very life. You must live the life only you can live. You are unique and valuable to this world. Live what is true for you, even with all the nay-sayers who claim it cannot be done. What do they know? Probably nothing that should keep you from doing what you must do. Whether it is starting a business, investing in a particular stock, or moving to a new city, it is your life to live. Own your ideas. Own your politics. Live for the principles, values, and beliefs that make sense to you and your philosophy of life. Above all, the point is to live it as you see fit. So dispel all of them who are pessimists for they are those who cannot see despite having eyes. Leave them behind because they will never add to your success. At this place in time, make your own decisions on who you will be and what you will do. Right or wrong, good or bad, it is your opportunity to strike out and find your purpose, your meaning, and your happiness. We go this way but once; it is not a dress rehearsal; it is the real thing. Do not squander it by being afraid. We are all afraid, searching in the darkness for the truth that we can call our own.

The essence of ownership, whether your skill, business, home, car, savings, ideas, or life itself, is your path to success. Wealth, health, security, and happiness can be maximized if you own these. If you rent, lease, borrow, or otherwise use what is not yours, it costs more, gives you less, and robs you of what could be yours. Renting is a temporary solution that usually makes others rich. You care more when it is yours to keep in the long run. And, it appears we are not going anywhere for a while, so why not own it for yourself?

"Life is never fair, and perhaps it is a good thing
for most of us that it is not."
Oscar Wilde

Chapter 8

Practical Money Tactics

Money contributes to security, well-being, and the ability to deal with problems that involve money, but it cannot make you happy. If it could, then the happiest people on Earth would be the super-wealthy. And judging by the number of divorces, cases of substance abuse, and suicides, it appears they are no more happy than people living in squalor. Although money might not make you happy, the lack of money almost certainly makes you miserable. In America, the first $10,000 dollars you make goes a long way towards improving your lot in life. However, each increment above that has less and less ability to deliver security, well-being, and an improved life in general. Lack of money and a large excess of money both have the power to ruin your life if you are not careful. It seems money is a double-edged sword capable of causing despair in the poor, destructive behavior in the rich, and significant worry for those in between.

The effect of money tends to magnify who you already are. A jerk without money is a bigger jerk with money. A Mother Teresa-type without money is strong and compassionate, but with money she is markedly stronger and more compassionate.

Escaping Minimum Wage

In the end though, money is merely a tool to be used whether for causes of good or motivations for ill gain. Do not be mistaken, however, money is important only because we say it is. It is an abstract idea, and its forms are merely junk metals and common paper worth nothing intrinsically. The meaning behind money is what makes it valuable.

Investment	Return	Time Period	Reference
U.S. Small Stocks`	13.1	1978-2008	1
Stamps: UK Penny Black	12.0	1980-2013	6
Coins: AU-50 Morgan Dollar	11.0	2009-2013	3
S & P 500	10.8	1978-2008	1
MSCI World Stocks	10.1	1978-2008	1
Business Real Estate	10.0	1978-2008	1
Long-term Treasury (20y)	9.8	1978-2008	1
Long-term Corporate Bond	9.1	1978-2008	1
Autographs: Abraham Lincoln	9.1	1946-2009	4
Farm Real Estate	8.8	1978-2008	1
S & P Commodity Index	7.8	1978-2008	1
1 Year Treasury	6.7	1978-2008	1
Art: Original Paintings	6.5	1963-2013	2
Residential Real Estate	5.7	1978-2008	1
Stamps: U.S. Scott #1	5.0	1950-2014	7
Stamps: U.S. Forever 1st Class	2.8	2007-2014	5
Coins: AU-50 Morgan Dollar	2.1	1980-2013	3
Lottery: $1.00 Scratch-Off	(80.0)	All	9
Lottery: Mega Millions	(88.9)	All	8

Reference 1: Francis, J.C., & Ibbotson, R.G. (2009). Journal of Portfolio Management, p 1-15, Fall 2009.
Reference 2: Korteimeg, Kraussl, & Verwijmeren (2013). www.gsb.stanford.edu/news/headlines/research-is-art-good-investment
Reference 3: www.us-coin-values-advisor.com
Reference 4: www.profilesinhistory.com/wp-content/uploads/2012/10/profiles_in_history_autograph_investment_guide.pdf
Reference 5: www.sentinelandenterprise.com/news/ci_24815011/are-forever-stamps-next-hot-investment
Reference 6: www.stampdomain.com/stamp_investment.html
Reference 7: www.stampdomain.com
Reference 8: www.getrichslowly.org/blog/2011/03/30/the-lottery-an-investment-for-fools-with-bonus-lottery-simulator/
Reference 9: www.getrichslowly.org/blog/2008/08/27/how-to-win-the-lottery/

Over the years Brian Tracy, a motivational teacher, has analyzed and worked with people on financial literacy. He found five main reasons why people do not achieve wealth. In addition, we have further examined some of these reasons.

It never occurred to you that you could become wealthy
Whether you never consider becoming wealthy or you do not think it is a possibility for you, the fact is you must believe you can achieve it. Often the non-wealthy have never had a wealthy role model nor even had any education about money and its nature. However, the required skills can be learned, and now more than ever the resources necessary can be found if desired.

Most of the non-wealthy never decide to become wealthy
They may think it is not possible or not practical for them to achieve true wealth. They maintain the status quo gleaned from whatever class their parents happened to be. This is very common and is very difficult to overcome because in essence it is how you think about money. Think differently and exciting things will happen.

Many of the non-wealthy procrastinate about money

Even if it occurs to you to become wealthy and you decide it is worthwhile to try, it still takes a conscious, sustained effort. If you delay and procrastinate long enough, it really won't matter if you decide to become wealthy because the opportunity dies a little each day. Make saving and investing a habit. If you cannot make it a habit, set up a process where some of your money flows to investments by default.

Many of the non-wealthy lack discipline

It takes more than a couple of years to amass wealth. In the meantime you must possess the focus necessary to put off instant gratification. Just because you have a little extra money does not mean you should buy whatever strikes your fancy. Consider thinking that the $50.00 spent on frivolous items is really worth $100.00 to yourself in five years.

Many of the non-wealthy only see the present moment

Consider taking a perspective on time that spans at least 5-7 years into your future. You will never regret saving and investing when you become the beneficiary at a point in the future.

Find any investment that suits you

You lose 100% of the money you fail to save. And if you factor in returns earned on your savings, you see losses of 110% per year. It is much more important to save in the beginning, later you can adjust in which vehicle you use. In the beginning do the best you can, and do not worry too much about fees and risk. Just get started.

Ruby Payne points out, "One of the biggest difficulties in getting out of poverty is managing money and just the general information base around money. How can you manage something you have never had?" Accordingly, there are five main money personalities that control how people relate to and use money. Often we adopt our parents' particular personality when it comes to money. And while this bond is fairly tight, once you identify which one you are like, you can make better choices going forward. Change is difficult because your money personality is something you acquire over many years beginning in your childhood. Nevertheless, with awareness you most decidedly can make that personality work for you.

Spender
   The spender is someone who derives great pleasure from buying things, services, and experiences. He tends to think that buying the next greatest thing will lead him to security and happiness. He tends to have much difficulty saving for times when money is tight. Often he cannot say no to a good deal whatever the price. Delaying gratification is non-existent. He tends to have too much month left and not enough cash. He has difficulty predicting future consequences of spending all his money today. He usually has nice things, like cars, homes and clothing, but also carries a lot of debt.

Saver
   The saver is someone who likes to retain large amounts of money. It brings him joy to see large numbers in his bank accounts. He is usually very conscientious and saves for the proverbial rainy-day. When others are broke and unable to take advantage of money situations, he comes through and reaps the rewards. He probably has difficulty spending large amounts of money even when it is perceived as a good thing, like buying a house or paying tuition.

Avoider
   The avoider is someone who dislikes the problems money management brings. These decisions, which must be made, cause him excessive anxiety. He would rather stick his head in the sand than deal with money problems. He tends to neglect money issues often because he does not understand how money works. He might have a love and hate relationship with his money.

Builder
   The builder accumulates large amounts of money. He spends a lot on investments. He uses his money for big projects most other people do not even dream of. Spending his money makes him feel powerful and important, a force inspiring awe by his peers. He may take risks, but they are well-calculated ones.

Escaping Minimum Wage

Rejecter
The rejecter hates money and the responsibility that comes with it. He thinks it corrupts. He thinks money is dirty and breeds contempt. He probably feels guilty for whatever amount of money he has even if earned honestly.

List of Practical Money Tactics
1. Work an additional job, but save 90% of what you earn from it. The point is not to just earn more, but to save this additional amount. If you are not careful, your level of spending will creep up to match your new income. Both, work and money spent, expand to fit current capacities.

2. Ask for a promotion every year on the job, or get a raise when you do something notable, then save 90% of it.

3. Be indispensable on the job and soon you will make more because you become worth it. Almost all businesses will reward its top producers and let attrition claim those who are not using their talents.

4. Make a lateral move to a better company, i.e., same job title but at a company worth your sacrifice. Often it is better to start at the bottom of a great company and work your way up, than it is to start in the middle of an average company and see no further benefit.

5. Change professions if you are in stepping-stone industries like, retail, hospitality, or personal services. If you desire more money and you are willing to do what is necessary to achieve it, use positions in retail, hospitality, and personal services only as fall-back positions. A fall-back position is a skill you possess like, cooking or janitorial, that you can easily go back to if you lose your main job. This way you have the ability to always bring in income no matter the economic health where you live.

6. Get your high school diploma or GED, and then get an apprenticeship, certificate, or associate degree. These set you apart from the 19 other applicants for the same job, and represent the minimum education necessary for a middle class existence.

7. Save excess money even if it is only 5 bucks. You lose 100% of the money you spend on stuff, i.e., junk. You lose 110% of the money you do not invest.

8. You will never be unhappy relying on money you have saved just for a certain problem or opportunity. It is a far better thing to save, sacrifice now, and be ready for opportunity, than to have a once-in-a-lifetime-opportunity present itself and find you have no resources.

9. Always have three to nine months of emergency savings. A man does not know what the day may bring.

10. For each major goal you make, open its own separate savings account. This way every dollar has a job to do in a certain place at a certain time.

11. Keep a journal for one month of all the money you spend or bring in during that month. This way you have a clear understanding how much you spend on unnecessary things like pizza, and can reassign spending to things you really want, like a newer car.

12. Rank all of your debt and investments by percent interest rate. Those with high rates get funded first. For example, if your credit card is at 16% and your stock investment is at 12%, then fund spending on both at the same time but with more going to the credit card. This way you eliminate debt faster while still enjoying watching your savings grow. Always pay down debt, which tends to be less fun, at the same time you fund savings, which tends to foster hope for a better future. Focusing solely on one or the other is not as productive.

13. For each savings-type account, make a coupon you pay each month just like it was a bill statement. Then pay it as you do for other bills. This works if you are not able to make saving automated, which is preferable.

14. Make a pay-off plan for each large expense. Know what dollars are going to it before you actually possess the dollars.

15. Be aware of compounding interest, which works against you in a mortgage or for you in a Roth IRA.

16. Monthly spending on debt/bills should equal about five to six percent of your yearly total. This represents a good rule of thumb to let you know how you are progressing.

17. Know why you are saving, investing, or spending. What do you want to do with your money?

18. Calculate your net worth each month. Examine how much is going towards interest, fees, and late charges, which give you no material gain. Make a ratio of debt to income, then aim to reduce all forms of debt, especially junk payments.

19. Keep 10% of all monies coming in. Keep 80% of all wind-fall payments, like rebates, tax returns, or bonuses. After all, you did not expect them in the first place, so keep as much as possible.

20. Know what activities bring in funds. Work is positive cash flow, but selling on eBay might not.

21. Invest in your ability to earn money. It is the way you will make a living. Purchase disability insurance over and above life insurance. Both are important, but disability is far more likely to happen than losing your life, at a young age. Insure your ability to earn money; it is a far greater thing than insuring stuff.

22. Work at a college to receive free or reduced tuition for yourself and your children.

23. Join the military and retire at age 38 with benefits, if you desire that. Otherwise you can join the Army to age 42, if you are in good health and desire that.

24. If you have difficulty getting your foot in the door at your dream job, volunteer at it instead. This way you learn the ropes and get to know the people who can hire you.

25. Go to a community college to get or start a degree, then transfer to a four-year school to get your bachelor's degree. You will save more than 50%, eventually possess two degrees, and enter the four-year school as a junior.

26. Diversify your skills. Use one as a fall-back position in case one does not work out.

27. Teach your hobby at the local vocational school.

28. Network even when you are not looking for a job. This way you can help others who are looking and assure that they will help you when you will be looking.

29. Get a roommate.

30. Define what you mean by wealth. When you have $X, then you know you are wealthy. Otherwise you never have an end game.

31. Wait to have children until you are established in a career, if you desire that.

32. Get a side-job you do for money under-the-table, like stump grinding or roofing.

33. Use your car sparingly and car-pool. Try to rely on public transportation if possible.

34. Work for a business that cannot be out-sourced to China.

35. Work for a business that can weather economic recessions.

36. After you earn a degree, keep it current with continued education.

37. Make savings and investments difficult to access, so you are less tempted to spend it and encouraged to reconsider your plans before spending it.

38. Expect some irregular expenses, like a dead battery or a unique opportunity.

39. Use a rewards credit card for all purchases, then pay it off at the next statement before interest is charged.

40. See a doctor, dentist, and eye doctor before you have problems. It is far easier to treat simple problems than it is to treat neglect of many years.

41. If not using a rewards credit card, pay with cash. Removing actual cash from your wallet makes you miss it and you will spend less.

42. Always make more than minimum payments when times are good.

43. Put off buying certain items. You might find you do not really want them or you can take advantage when they are reduced in a sale.

44. Manage your credit report. Dispute errors. Know what your FICO score is, so you know what activities help or hurt it.

45. Donate to your charity, church, or alma mater. There are others likely to be less well-off than you are at the moment. Clint Murchison's father is claimed to have said, "Money is like manure. If you spread it around it does a lot of good. But if you pile it up in one place, it stinks like hell."

46. Do not declare bankruptcy unless forced to by your creditors. Almost all credit is extended based on your FICO score, and a bankruptcy destroys your score for ten years.

47. Purchase term life insurance to cover your income, especially if you have a spouse and children.

48. Remember that 80% of all self-made millionaires are entrepreneurs or salespeople.

49. If you think you have no money to save now, think how much less you will have four years from now. Chances are you will be somewhere in four years; why not be there with a little money to spend. If you cannot save, then you deserve to be poor.

50. Have good reasons why you spend money. If you really enjoy a particular brand of expensive coffee, do not feel bad spending your hard earned money on it. After all, money is meant to be spent. Consider Philander C. Johnson in *Senator Sorghum's Primer of Politics* (1906) that, "A man fails to appreciate the value of money when he holds on to it so tight that he gets no benefit from it."

51. Avoid pay-day loans and credit cards. The interest is simply too great.

52. Your FICO score is composed of: punctuality of payment, amount of debt, length of time of open status, new credit requested, and mixture of credit types.

53. Donate to charity, religion, or alma mater

"Our truest life is when we are in dreams awake."
Henry David Thoreau

Escaping Minimum Wage

Questions to ask yourself
1. Why do you want to be out of debt?
2. Why do you want to save?
3. Why do you want to invest your money?
4. What do you want in your life that money can buy?
5. Why are you in debt?
6. Why have you not begun to save regularly?
7. How much debt do you have?
8. How much is your income?
9. How much do you pay in interest and fees?
10. What is the worst thing that could happen if I fail to save?
11. What is my current net worth?
12. How will you know when you have enough money?
13. What is your definition of a good life with money?

As potent as money is, most people tend to worship or demonize it. In both cases, they fail to do what should be done: to use money for the betterment of their own lives and the lives of others. Fiscal responsibility eludes many, but for a select few who concentrate on it the rewards are great. For the masses, however, never before have we had so much stuff and so little time to enjoy it. Servicing the debt on things we do not really care about is forcing us to work longer and harder. Just take a look at how many storage buildings that can be rented in any town. Luck, IQ, and inheritance do not explain how those who amass wealth have done it. The truth of the matter is they learn the principles of how to amass wealth, and then focus their actions on them. This is good news because this means almost everyone can learn these principles in several hours of study. Then, it is just a matter of discipline to engage them and persist until wealth is achieved.

"The privilege of a lifetime is being who you are."
Joseph Campbell

Chapter 9

Remedies by the Individual

(Listed in order of Strength)

In escaping minimum wage, the very best single thing you can do is to get your high school diploma or GED. Almost all employers want candidates who have shown enough drive and ability to graduate high school, and those who have dropped out for whatever reason are not highly regarded. A high school diploma probably does not open as many doors as a higher degree does, but without it many doors are effectively closed. Graduating high school is the minimum standard by which all candidates are measured against at first look. A high school degree demonstrates you can undertake a challenge and complete it satisfactorily. Additionally, a high school diploma signals to the employer that you can read, write, compute, and communicate on a level necessary for success at a minimum. In your efforts to escape minimum wage, the worst thing you could do is to present yourself as unable to complete this first educational credential. Without it, you will find the jobs available to you are as limited as your inability to achieve a diploma. Better candidates get better jobs, and the rest are relegated to entry-level positions.

Post-High School Training

Once you have a high school diploma or GED, it is highly recommended that you complete some sort of specialized career training if you want to progress beyond highly prescribed, low wage work. This training could be a post-secondary certificate, apprenticeship, volunteer work, associate degree or training on-the-job. All of these are good second steps to more interesting work that is in demand where you live. Notice that these well-esteemed jobs do not require bachelor degrees or higher. In fact, many bachelor degree candidates end up being underemployed simply because there are not enough good jobs for all bachelor degree holders. Many successful candidates end formal education with one of these credentials, and they go on to do well in the labor market. You might consider jobs like licensed practical nursing, dental assistant, cosmetologist, or any of the trades. These types of credentials lead to jobs that pay more than minimum wage, often much more, and go a long way to differentiating yourself from those with only a high school diploma. Plus, a post-secondary credential signals to the employer that you are motivated, responsible, possess specialized knowledge, and desire to perform well on the job. Employers are willing to pay for these skills because they know from experience that previous incumbents with similar credentials have been much more productive and capable than those with only a high school diploma or less. The major function of an adult in America is to work. And given that you will spend 40 years at work, it is advantageous to do something you like that also pays well. After all, as Brian Tracy, the motivational speaker, said, "working at something you don't care about is the very best way to waste your life." So we come to the conclusion that it is best to graduate high school and then complete some sort of post-secondary training of your choice to earn more than minimum wage for your entire working career.

Avoid Industries Paying MW & Find a High-Quality Company

When looking for work, avoid industries that employ the lion share of minimum wage incumbents. These are hospitality (e.g., hotels), food service, personal services, and unskilled labor. Just by avoiding these, you greatly increase your chances of earning more than minimum wages. The second thing to do is to search for a position in a high quality company or organization. Look for companies that have good reputations, steady earnings, and satisfied workers. Get any job in one of these employers, even if it is part-time, temporary, an internship, a volunteer position, or not exactly what you want at this point. Soon enough, if you demonstrate productivity and a positive mental attitude, you will be asked to do more. He who does the small things well will be entrusted with bigger things in short order. It was Jonas Salk who rightly claimed, "The reward for work well done is the opportunity to do more."

Know Your Talent & Exploit It

Examine, and know yourself. Understand that being in poverty and working for minimum wage is rarely about lack of intelligence. Most people have enough intellect to do a wide range of jobs. It also is not about talent. Everyone has a given talent that is capable of carrying her to the success she desires. Long ago someone said talent is as common as salt. The problem, of course, is finding that talent, and then getting people to pay you for the products of your talent. To summarize, finding an outlet for your best talent that people will pay for is the essence of work.

Work Full-time on a Good Opportunity

Another good way to escape minimum wage is to work full-time at a job with fringe benefits. This might seem overly simplistic, but the fact is a lot of people who work for minimum wage do not work full-time. This characteristic has been found when looking at why some incumbents have so much while others have so little. Despite this, do not interpret this to mean that those who work for minimum wage are lazy. Incumbents working for minimum wage work very hard, sometimes much harder than the people above them. The point is, however, working full-time, day in and day out, will pay off in better opportunities, if only because you are there and ready to receive it when it happens.

Have More than One Skill

Diversifying your revenue stream can also lift you out of poverty and minimum wage. Essentially this means to have more than one marketable skill so you always have options. For example, your primary job might be a shift manager at a fast food restaurant, but you also sell used electronics on Ebay. If one or the other stops producing income, you have the other one to pick up the slack. This is your fall-back position.

Move to Where the Jobs Are

Where you live has ramifications on where you work. Not every profession is viable in every location. To overcome this, you should carefully consider the local employability of your postsecondary credential. It helps to begin your training with an eye on the end result. Ask yourself for instance, if I get an education in aeronautical technology is there a place to employ me when I graduate. You may want to move to a stronger metropolitan area, say from Youngstown, Ohio to Columbus, Ohio or from Norfolk, Virginia to Washington D.C. to take two examples.

Trust Your Little Voice

Learn to rely on yourself. What you become in life is much more a product of what you choose to do than anything else. Avoid being made the victim. Take responsibility for your life, and not when you come to die find that you have not lived. Prepare for opportunity. It will come but once. If you do not know where to start with all of this, you will never go wrong honing your purpose, that thing that excites you to action. Most of all, be clear about what you want and who you want to become. Forming a good question about what your life's purpose makes answering it easy. And once clear, you have a path to follow.

Set Exciting Goals with Purpose

From your purpose, it is elementary to craft your goals. Setting goals and working toward them is something the successful do. The best way to fail is to ignore setting goals. Doing so, you drift making no progress towards any destination worthwhile. Write down you goals, and then rewrite them each day until you accomplish them. This way they stay fresh in your mind. If you do these two actions, you will achieve more, and achieve it faster. Live in the moment, but be sure to be cognizant of the future. Spending too much time in the moment causes you to forget your purpose whereas spending too much time on the future makes the present worthless, and therein, neither is taken care of .

It's a Choice You Make Not Something Thrust Upon You

Many incumbents remain in poverty earning minimum wages because they do not know that it is a choice they make each day. And if they happen to know that it is a choice, they have no one to guide them on the way. More often than not, it takes someone to come along side them and offer encouragement. Parents do this, but if they do not then the schools must. But the good thing is that almost anyone can add value to another with just a little time and sincere effort.

Planning Sets Up Good Choices

Good planning is vital. If someone cannot plan, then he cannot predict outcomes. If he cannot predict, then he cannot learn cause and effect. If he cannot understand cause and effect, then he cannot identify consequences. If he cannot determine consequences, then he cannot control his impulsivity. And if he cannot control his impulses, then he is likely to make poor choices, which have all kinds of problems.

Avoid Teenage Pregnancy

The order in which one lives her life has real consequences. Teenage pregnancy often leads to single parenting. This event forces her to play her hand differently than if she had waited to have children until married. It can have disastrous effects on her career because she needs to support her children immediately with whatever job she can obtain. Also, It is beneficial to have children and get married at an older age, where she is probably more mature and better able to parent.

Mind Your Health but Get Disability Insurance

Take care of your health. If you cannot work due to poor health, how can you make a comfortable living? Disability insurance is far more important and likely to be used than life insurance. Automobile accidents tend to mangle its victims leading to disability instead of bluntly killing them. Your ability to earn money from work is how most people survive, so you are well advised to insure it. This is more important as you earn progressively more money.

Good Parenting Sets the Table for Future Success

Parenting imparts much more than just genetics. A child is very likely to turn out like her parents. This bond is at least as strong as educational achievement. Good parenting is warm, but with enough discipline. It is intellectually stimulating. It makes an environment that is emotionally and financially secure. And perhaps most importantly, good parenting offers effective guidance where they together identify and develop the child's best talent so she has a firm sense of identity and purpose. Nothing can take the place of good parenting, even though the schools try.

Make Strong Relationships

From Ruby Payne's book mentioned earlier, she finds, "When students who have been in poverty (and have successfully made it into middle class) are asked how they made the journey, the answer nine times out of ten has to do with a relationship – a teacher, counselor, or coach who made a suggestion or took an interest in them as individuals." This fact is true not only for the poor, but also, for everyone looking to improve his lot in life. A key relationship, whether a mentor or network contact, is how most people achieve success in the world of work.

Become a Salesperson or Entrepreneur

Start a business around your best talent if you are so inclined. Most self-made millionaires (about 80%) are either small business owners (i.e., entrepreneurs) or salespeople.

Keep It Legal

Avoid illegal drugs, alcohol, crime, and violence. Any of these have the power to permanently cripple your life and career. With convictions involving these, you are barred from entering certain professions. For example, a drug conviction bars you from becoming a K-12 teacher.

> "Success is not final, failure is not fatal:
> It is the courage to continue that counts."
> Winston Churchill

Take Ownership

Save your money. You will never be unhappy falling back on money you have saved for just this purpose. Purchase ownership of assets, like a credential, home, or business. Owning these and others like them tend to open more possibilities than if you just "rent" them. Neither a lender nor borrower be. Both put you at risk. Not being repaid in the former, and being charged outrageous interest that compounds against you in the latter.

Have Something to Do Outside of Work

Use all of your paid vacation days. Spend this free time on a hobby, and who knows, it might turn into a full-time engagement.

Summary

Begin with education, find your talent, then do some type of work full-time that will sustain you financially and that you find interesting. Develop more than one skill so you have more than one revenue stream. Avoid teenage pregnancy, early marriage, and all things destructive, like drugs, alcohol, illegal activities or procrastination. Plan, set good goals, and trust yourself to make bold decisions, like moving to a robust locality to take a job with a strong organization. Know that you can do it; and, your very belief of this will make it come true.

Conclusions

Remember you are the author of your life, no one else can do it for you. Get the education, find the skills, move if you have to, but remember all you have to do find that singular opportunity that dwarfs all others *in your view*. If you do just a few of the remedies given here, you will be well ahead and on a good trajectory for success in due time. Good things will happen; it is your responsibility to be ready to take advantage when they do.

> "Doing what you love is the cornerstone
> of having abundance in your life."
> Wayne Dyer

"It is far more important to do
what is right than what is enjoyable."
Phillip D. Taylor

Chapter 10

Remedies by Society

Raising the minimum wage and then pegging it to annual increases in the Consumer Price Index (CPI) is the best remedy we can hope for. No one expects to get rich working for minimum wage, but it should be a dignified and productive way of contributing and making an honest living. As it stands now, it accomplishes none of these. Despite full-time work, those working for MW have to rely on handouts from the government to make ends meet. In fact, companies paying only minimum wage effectively get a subsidy to keep wages low because they know the government will provide their under-paid incumbents with benefits like food assistance and healthcare discounts. This is not a dignified way to reward work behavior that, as we all agree, is what we want every able-bodied adult to do. Minimum wage does not reward increasing productivity. After all, why would incumbents strive to be the best at what they do if all they ever got were low pay with no raises and a pittance from the government. Again, we are not rewarding the behavior we want, and in doing so, we actually promote the behavior we do not want. That is, dependence, lack of initiative, and passivity.

How Much is Enough

Years of inflation without corresponding increases in the MW act very much like a regressive tax hitting the poor much harder than what the middle class or rich face. The first ten thousand dollars one makes goes a long way to improving her life. Each increment after that has less and less ability to add to her standard of living. Economists have discovered that happiness increases as one earns more money up to about $75,000. After that, more money does not add proportional gains in happiness and well-being. There is a reason why the government has come up with the definition of poverty. The poverty line describes the minimum an incumbent needs to provide the healthful-basics of life, such as home, food, clothing, and healthcare. As said before, the minimum wage should be that wage that enables any man or woman to take care of these basics without any government assistance.

The Economic Policy Institute found that if the MW was boosted from its current level of $7.25 per hour to $10.10, as proposed by the Fair Minimum Wage Act of 2014, more than 1.7 million Americans would no longer have to rely on public assistance programs. This change alone would produce $7.6 billion per year in savings to the federal government, a large number, but just a drop in our collective-bucket. This is good news unless you are a fast food restaurant or large hotel. The $7.6 billion has to come from somewhere, and in this case it goes from public entitlements to private paychecks, and herein we find a problem. What was once paid for by the government now must be paid out of revenue from companies that employ large numbers of MW incumbents. In effect, it would act like an ill distributed tax on these employers. This change has little effect on a company like GE whereas its effect on a company like YUM Brands is much greater. In the end though, the costs to the latter are likely to be transferred to the consumer. This is acceptable financially and morally.

Increase Tax on Capital Gains and Lower It on Labor Income

If the government would increases taxes on capital gains and dividends while simultaneously lowering taxes on income from labor, this would place the emphasis of the tax on behavior we want to foster. There is little logic in taxing someone 15% on capital gains that is entirely passive while someone earning $35,000 would be taxed at, say, 24% that came from hard work. Remember we get more of what we subsidize and we get more of what we reward. As it is now, we reward investing over working, so the poor get left behind at no fault of there own.

Need-Based Aid for College Education

A bachelor degree has been likened to a passport to the middle class, albeit rather tritely. A college education used to be the sure-fire way of achieving money and status in America. However, this position is increasingly being priced out of reach by incumbents in MW jobs. It is no secret that tuition has been rising in double digits for many years now. As states have withdrawn support, more of the cost of a college education has been transferred to the student. This event is logical because it is the student that increasingly reaps the rewards of getting an education. However, at the same time, need-based aid, such as the Pell Grant and state grants, has decreased. In the 1970s it was possible for a student with little familial resources to use grants to pay for an entire four-year education, but today this is virtually impossible.

These two events (i.e., increases in tuition and much lower need-based aid) mean MW workers have enormous difficulties paying for college. We see students stopping-out due to financial pressures. We see candidates that never even try to get an education because they are so disillusioned with the reality of large student loans. We see students trying unsuccessfully to work, study, and have a family all at the same time. We see the huge burden of student loans on students who have left early without a degree. They do not get the advantage of the degree, yet owe for it anyhow. What we see from all this is more students with adequate familial resources (e.g., the middle class and rich) go to college and graduate, but also, we see the lower income students going and graduating only by carrying large amounts of debt with the hopes of it paying off. This situation will work, albeit inefficiently, as long as college graduates get high paying jobs specifically from the knowledge, skill, ability, and network contacts gained from their bachelor degree. If college graduates are for any reason, not rewarded for their time, effort, and money spent, the whole system comes crashing down. And then and only then will things change.

money than their peers left behind in MW jobs even though with some encouragement and support they too could realize such gains.

Let Poor Accumulate Assets

Government could restructure its qualifications for public aid in an effort to encourage MW workers to obtain important assets. For instance, they might be allowed to accumulate assets, like a primary home or considerable savings, without losing benefits. It is far more fair to overpay government benefits for a time, than to cut off recipients early before they have made real progress. The poor who work for MW spend every last dime that they earn. This means they are always in the stressors of the present challenge, and despite wanting to save and invest for the future, they cannot. Without an excess of income that is valued as a future benefit, they will not save, regardless of the amount. Some people just spend it all. Some do so because they really do not have anything left over, while others who could save a little do not value doing that. The problem is separating the two. We do not want to encourage dependence when they might be making enough to well without it. It seems in the final analysis though, assets definitely must impact government assistance programs, but the restrictions should be eased somewhat. Being permitted to save and invest, whether in skills or simply in financial instruments, means those working for MW have a real, viable path to achieving more. If they see it as a real future for them, they will see it as achievable. And it is with this added motivation that they will overcome being pigeon-holed into MW jobs, a tangible benefit for them and a boon for the greater economy. This is consistent with encouraging behaviors that Americans value.

Small Business Creation

Entrepreneurship should be encouraged. Many who would take on the risk of owning and operating a business do not do so for just a few reasons. First the risk of losing it all financially is very real. Second, they simply do not know how, and if they know how they lack necessary resources. Finally, the maze of legal requirements is daunting. The process is not difficult, but it is very hard to find the way. Starting a business should be easy. Educational support is key because working with someone who has done it before provides much benefit. The government could be so good at this if it really tried. This would be much more productive than studying how fruit-flies react to alcohol, for example. MW workers could band together and start any sort of successful franchise. They do not know it, they already possess many skills required by entrepreneurs, and if they do know it, they have left their peers behind. Streamlining the administrative process, providing knowledge support, and perhaps, funding a portion of the venture would go a long way in helping disenfranchised MW incumbents create a future they want to live in.

A Two Tiered Minimum Wage

Some businesses in certain industries (e.g., hospitality, unskilled labor, and retailing) seem overly sensitive to increasing the minimum wage. They see it as dramatically increasing their labor costs instead of empowering their incumbents to produce more and in turn spend more throughout the economy. To rectify this somewhat, a two tier system would make sense. The first tier would consist of incumbents who have little or no work experience. The second tier would consist of all incumbents with a certain level of experience or educational attainment. Importantly, these tiers are not based on age, even though many in the first tier would be young. A fair way of dividing the experienced from the inexperienced is to consider how many Social Security credits one has earned. In 2014, an incumbent earns one credit for each $1,200 increment of earnings up to a maximum of four per year. The amount one credit costs goes up slightly each year. Using this definition, an inexperienced incumbent would earn say, $7.25 per hour, and need to earn eight credits or an Associate degree before progressing to the second tier where she would make at least say, $10.10. This assures that business pays its incumbents based on experience, and probably, for their productivity.

This small change encourages behavior we desire from a knowledgeable, progressing workforce. Two such examples are less turnover of inexperienced workers, and fostering desire to get at least an Associate degree. This change would also mean businesses that use a lot of MW incumbents would favor hiring candidates with no experience.

Thus, when taken in the aggregate, this would help many on to the lower rungs of the career ladder, who might not have otherwise bothered to seek employment. This results in both a stronger workforce and a more robust economy at little additional expense.

Reward Business for Full-time , Full-benefit Job Creation

It would be good for business to be rewarded for the total number of full-time, full-benefit positions it creates in a year. The reward could be a tax rebate or other tax advantage. We could also penalize companies that cut full-time, full-benefit jobs by the same metric. Importantly, this includes those companies off-shoring good American jobs, and would encourage their retention here in the fifty states. It would also encourage the consolidation of part-time positions into groupings of full-time, full-benefit incumbents. We want better jobs for all candidates. By producing more full-time, full-benefit positions, more incumbents share in this advantage. Of course, part-time jobs have their place, and they might see reductions and lower availability, but this loss would be more than made up for by advancing those who can and will work full-time, especially those who work MW jobs. To put it frankly, it is better to employ one full-time, full-benefit father with three children and a wife, than two or three part-time teenagers who have no dependents and little obligations. A tax advantage like this promotes how we want work in America to be.

Double the Earned Income Tax Credit

The Earned Income Tax Credit is a government benefit worthy of aggressive expansion and reach. The EITC pays low income incumbents a benefit dependent on how much they earn in a given year. Low income, single parents see this as very positive because it rewards their hard work, often in MW jobs. Presidents from both sides of the aisle have favored it. Democrats see it as helping their low income constituents, while the Republicans see it as rewarding work and independence. The EITC in many ways is more fair than a MW increase, but the important thing to remember is that it promotes candidates to work, who may be marginally attached to the workforce and earn MW. Doubling this benefit, even if other programs have to be cut, might see wide approval among Democrats, Republicans, and American taxpayers in addition to the recipients. One thing for sure is that America despises giving away government entitlements to people who have not earned it, and in this case they surely have earned it.

Subsidize Early Childhood Education

Learning begins long before Kindergarten. Early childhood education (i.e., pre-K) helps all children, but it helps those children who come from disadvantaged homes much more than more affluent children. Disadvantaged children fall way behind if education is not started way before Kindergarten. Even though formal schooling tends to move everyone along at similar rates, there is ample, clear evidence that shows more affluent children invariably do better. This type of deficit may exist and accelerate as the grades pass by. One often cited statistic is that by graduation of high school the white child, who had early childhood education and satisfactory home resources, is four grades ahead of the black child, who did not have early childhood education and satisfactory home resources. Clearly this is not what was intended, and yet it is reality. Because of findings like this, it is important to subsidize early childhood education, especially for children at risk.

"Don't aim for success if you want it; just do what you love and believe in, and it will come naturally."
David Frost

"Work in its entirety is finding an outlet
for your best talent that someone will pay for."
Phillip D. Taylor

Appendix A

"How do you find purpose in your life?"

Finding Purpose

Adam Leipzig on YouTube.com says it is simple once you ask the right questions. Here we focus on just careers, but you could just as easily do it for life in general. He is right because a well-crafted question almost answers itself. Once you concentrate your efforts in the right direction the answers become easy.

Start with a little introspection.

    Who are you?
    What are you passionate about?
    What are your deepest held values?
    How are you unique?

Life and work is not just about existing or being, rather, it is what you do, or your essence. The reason why you work.

    What do you do?

It is not enough to do just for yourself, although that is important. Who can you help through your work? Who do you serve with your unique talent?

Digging deeper; what is it that they need or want from you? What product, service, or experience can you best serve them? And finally, how do they change, develop, or gain from what you have provided?

Let us summarize and give a quick example.

1. **Who are you? Existence:**
    "I am Phil."

2. **What do you do? Essence:**
    "I write and assist."

3. **Where do I do my work? Location:**
    "At my home office & over the internet"

4. **Who do you serve? Who:**
    "I serve job seekers."

5. **What do they need from me? How to Serve:**
    "They need suitable work."

6. **How do they change because of me? Value given:**
    "They gain a productive, meaningful career."

"My life is my message."
Mahatma Gandhi

Appendix B

Decision Making

Decision-making is difficult. It is even more so when the decision concerns your immediate and long-term futures. Deciding on a career is one of those futures. Here at the beginning, it is necessary to help put you at ease. A decision on major or career can be changed. But more importantly, you will probably get it right in the end. Chances are once you dig deep, reflect, gather some information, and trust your heart and gut, you will find you have always had a strong inkling for your perfect career even if right now you are confused and anxious. It is sort of like Dorothy in the Wizard of Oz; she had the power all along but just needed a little courage and a reminder. Of course, with a decision this big there are natural anxieties, and it may take some time, but the answer is there.

What we have to do to make a good career choice is to understand that there will always be uncertainties, complexities, and risks to any choice of action, but I assure you the risks of not engaging in this discussion far outweigh any "bad" choice you could make. Yes, some facts will always elude you. Yes, there are numerous factors to consider. And yes, there are risks, some you see and some you do not. The future by its very definition is undefined; however, with careful thought and bounded emotion you can reduce the anxiety as you get there. What comes below is a clear process hopefully leading to consistent, ordered, and reasoned decisions on your journey to making a living.

Creating a conducive atmosphere for inquiry
Focus:

The very first thing you need to help you choose a career is to focus on the task at hand. What you focus on is what gets solved. Be sure to focus more on your career decision than the focus you put into going on vacation. It takes thought and reflection to make a good choice. The vacation may be a lot of fun and is worthwhile to plan, but it is crucial to spend enough time asking questions, getting feedback, and trying things on for that activity that will consume 50 or more hours every week, week after week. Make a poor decision, such as working for the money, and life becomes drudgery, but make a good choice and life becomes a recreational pursuit, a labor of love. So to start, remove all distractions, such as uninvolved others and anything that competes for your time. And then begin, because if we wait until everything is ready, we shall never begin. So live the life you have imagined and the future you see is the future you will get.

Eliminate excessive emotion:

Eliminate as much excess emotion as possible and use as much logic a you can muster. Strong emotion has a way of coloring your thoughts so you see something not quite true. These emotions often elicit decisions out of fear or greed. This fact is played out everyday on the stock market. Do not worry there will be a time later on when you will need to rely on your emotions. But for now, you need a clear head. It may help to change your environment to a place where you can think and reflect, perhaps, a walk in the woods or feeding the ducks at the park will give you the time and space you need.

Procrastinate

Procrastination is not always harmful. It serves a purpose, otherwise we would not engage in it. In this context, its purpose is to give you time to gather more information, evaluate and reflect. You should always be able to procrastinate when you cannot make an immediate decision. This action helps you stay fresh; it helps you develop perspective and insight. Never be afraid to put off any big decision. Think of it as a space shuttle launch where the countdown is halted at 14 seconds due to an unknown problem. In your case and that of NASA, a delay can avoid catastrophe. Procrastinate on purpose in order to rejuvenate without guilt.

Establish the objective:

An objective is the vision, an end state in this example. Know what you want to achieve from this process. Think of this similarly to the function of a compass. It tells you the direction, but not how to go about getting there. For instance in this context, the objective is to uncover a career you will excel in, enjoy, and add value to others. It says nothing of the multitude of ways to actually make this happen.

The question:

Generate a question that is accurately stated. It must be clear, compelling, and of your own design. Asking the right question goes a long way towards getting the right answer. Take the advice of Charles F. Kettering that, "a problem well stated is a problem half solved." Be sure to include all the necessary parameters and qualifiers. There is nothing worse than working hard to get a good answer only to get to the end and discover you have answered the wrong question. This is the difference between going 70 mph towards Indianapolis when you should be going 70 mph towards Denver, the right road maybe, but the wrong direction entirely.

Outline who is directly and indirectly involved in the decision

Ask yourself, "Who will this decision affect?" Of course, it affects you, which is one thing, but if it affects others that is quite different. When others must be included in your decision-making, it often quickly compounds the decision. What was once an easy decision can suddenly become complex and convoluted. If this is the case, you have a duty to ask for their input.

Be open and receptive

It behooves you to be open and ready to receive whatever your best logic and guarded emotion can deliver. When you start this process, check your closed-mind, and that of significant others, at the door. There is no room for pessimism for a closed mind brings nothing but obstacle, negativity, and an "I-Can't" attitude. In this respect, it is your responsibility to bring courage, focus, and openness to bear on the problem at hand as if an eager child on the first day of Kindergarten.

Generate good options by brainstorming:

A good decision must take into consideration as many possible and probable alternatives. Omitting several can result in a mediocre result. Look at the problem from many perspectives. If deciding on a career, you might want to consider aspects such as how you will do the job in 20 years or how appropriate the choice is for that location. You may ask yourself is this career growing and diversifying or has it matured and declining.

Brainstorming is a common technique where a lot of ideas are generated in a short time. It consists of writing down every idea that comes to mind for a set period of time, say 10 minutes. The quality, feasibility and applicability are ignored. These are evaluated later upon review. It helps to have someone do this with you to generate the most responses.

Reverse Brainstorming is the process of generating ideas that are contrary to what is desired. This process is valuable because it uncovers opposites which can then be turned around to give insight as what not to do and what to do. It gives a different perspective and yields more and different results. When you do this for making a career decision, often you will come across interesting careers you may not have otherwise thought of. But most of the time, you will generate careers that have something in common, which you must tease out.

Exploring the different options

Once you have generated a large pool of options, you then need to evaluate each one on its merits, such as feasibility, risk/reward, uncertainty, and potential implications. In choosing a career, risk comes in the form of wasted time and money, unemployment and underemployment after graduation, excessive educational cost and high opportunity cost, and incongruence between personality and career. These risks can reasonably be reduced by doing research (e.g., reading, taking tests), getting experiential knowledge (e.g., internship, co-op) and assessing threats (e.g., growing vs. declining) and how to overcome them before they happen.

Choosing the Best Option

Once you have explored all the best options, it is time to choose among them. Unless you have already narrowed the field to a single choice, Grid Analysis is a very powerful tool to narrow the best choices to one or two. See pages 158 and 160 for a completed grid and a blank one for your use. The grid is explained in detail on those pages, but briefly it is the process of assigning each variable a weighted, numerical score that is totaled for each career in question.

Just as you select the appropriate plan of action, you should also create a back-up plan, a contingency plan, an escape hatch you can fall back on should your planning fail you. After all, it was General Eisenhower who said in getting ready for the D-Day invasion, "In preparing for battle, I have always found that plans are useless, but planning is indispensable." How else are you to become familiar with yourself, your abilities, strengths and weaknesses? What if you do not get into medical school, what if you run out of money for college, or what if you discover what you thought is not actually the way it is?

Finally, some common wisdom from the Internet, "If you find that you have to talk yourself into a decision, it is usually a bad decision," "Make the small decisions with your head and the big ones with your heart," "Imagine having made a final decision. If you get a feeling of relief, that is the way to go, even if it is coupled with a little sadness," and "Let go of fear. Know there is no right or wrong decision. Any decision is better than indecision."

"Success consists of going from
failure to failure without loss of enthusiasm."
Winston Churchill

Appendix C

Grid Analysis

How to measure and evaluate
several career possibilities

Appendix C: Figure 1-1: Example Grid Analysis for three occupations against Six Variables. All scores are 0-5.

Chosen Characteristics	Wt	Physics Teacher		Chemical Engineer		Nuclear Engineer	
Work with People	4X	5	20	3	12	2	8
Match with Holland's Code	5X	5	25	5	25	5	25
Breadth of employment	3X	4	12	4	12	2	6
Physical Demands	5X	5	25	3	15	3	15
Prestige	3X	2	6	4	12	4	12
Ratio of Jobs to Degrees	5X	3	15	2	10	5	25
Total			103		86		91
Percent of Match			69%		57%		61%

Rank: A perfect score is 150.
    1st = Physics Teacher
    2nd = Nuclear Engineer
    3rd = Chemical Engineer

Directions to Appendix C: Figure 1

From the grid above, each job characteristic is weighted relative to a 0-5 point scale where 0 is low and 5 is high. This hypothetical person chose to put extra weight on Holland's Code, Physical Demands, and Ratio of Jobs to Degrees because she determined those factors to be most important to her career success. Notice that the weightings do not have to be different, but they can be. See Appendix C, page 159, for list of possible characteristics.

Next, each occupation is scored on a 0-5 scale where 0 is low and 5 is high for its importance relative to that particular job characteristic. To arrive at what value to assign to a particular career characteristic, it requires you to do some research, beginning with the Occupational Outlook Handbook published by the U.S. Department of Labor and/or other career reference books. Once you review each selected occupation in these books, you are ready to assign relative scores. Notice that the scores vary from occupation to occupation.

Multiply the weight multiplier (0-5) by the raw score (0-5) for each characteristic to arrive at the product. Finally, all of the products are totaled for each occupation in the vertical column. Higher totals indicate a stronger match to what you value in a career. If you have more characteristics to evaluate or have more than three occupations, simply expand the grid to include all the variables you desire.

Interpretation

From the grid we see that the best match is Physics Teacher, then Nuclear Engineer, followed by Chemical Engineer. You can see that these occupations are closely related. This emphasizes the congruence and agreement of this person's personality, interests, and values with the demands of these occupations. If she were a college student and was undecided about a major even with this analysis, she would be safe in taking courses that are common to all three, such as Algebra, Calculus, Physics 1, Physics 2, Chemistry 1 and Chemistry 2. This sort of procrastination affords her more time to explore, gather information, go on shadow experiences, volunteer in high schools, do informational interviews, and evaluate other aspects, such as geographic opportunities and salary of these occupations.

Escaping Minimum Wage

Selected Characteristics	Wt	1:	2:	3:
Total				
Percent Match				

List of Possible Career Characteristics
- Prestige
- Salary
- Location
- Work with People
- Work with Things
- Work with Data
- Work with Ideas
- Education Requirements
- Match with Holland Codes
  - Realistic
  - Investigative
  - Social
  - Enterprising
  - Conventional
  - Artistic
- Breadth of Employment
- Physical Demands
- Emotional Demands
- Requires Work Outside of Work
- Ratio of Jobs to Degrees
- Length of Educational Training
- Cost of Skill Training
- Rate of Unemployment
- Personality Match
- Amount of Travel Required
- Commute Time
- Shift Worked
- Use of Your Strengths
- Full or Part-time
- Temporary or Permanent
- Relationship with Coworkers
- Autonomy
- Responsibility
- Challenge
- Fulfills Purpose & Major Life Goals

About the Author

Phillip D. Taylor received his Bachelor Degree from Kent State University in 1996 and his Master Degree in College Administration from The University of Akron in 2004. This book is preceded by his inaugural work, *The First Step before a Thousand: Career Planning 2014-2015*. His first job was at Long John Silvers, where he made Minimum Wage and received one 10 cent raise in three years. He has also worked at or near Minimum Wage, as a night janitor, nursing assistant, and office clerk. These intellectually impoverished positions motivated him to go back to school. He now considers himself to be among the middle class, if not for the money he makes, but instead for the skill and education he uses, which is writing books. He encourages you to submit articles or otherwise contact him at: ProLineCareers@gmail.com.

"Nothing ever goes away until it
teaches us what we need to know."
Pema Chodron

www.ingramcontent.com/pod-product-compliance
Lightning Source LLC
Chambersburg PA
CBHW080249180526
45167CB00006B/2471